1001
Basketball
Trivia Questions

Dale Ratermann
Brian Brosi

Sports Publishing Inc.
www.SportsPublishingInc.com

A **SPORTS**MASTERS Book

Editor: Susan M. McKinney
Project manager, book design: Jennifer L. Polson
Cover design: Scot Muncaster

ISBN: 1-58382-014-0
Library of Congress number: 99-60723

Printed in the United States.

Sports Publishing Inc.
A Sports Masters Press book
www.SportsPublishingInc.com

Acknowledgments

Thank you to Dreaming Dog Publishing for negotiating the deal to get this collection in print.

Thank you to Tom Bast and Tom Doherty at SPORTSMASTERS Press, Peter Bannon, Mike Pearson and designer Jennifer Polson of Sports Publishing Inc.

And thank you to the teams and schools that contributed photographs.

Contents

THE NBA AND ITS TEAMS

Q.

1. Name each of the five previous names of the Washington Wizards.

Washington Bullets, Capital Bullets, Baltimore Bullets, Chicago Zephyrs and Chicago Packers.

2. What team hired Florence Griffith-Joyner to design its uniforms?

Indiana Pacers.

3. The Houston Rockets of 1978-79 is the only team to have four players shoot better than 85 percent from the free throw line. Name the players.

Mike Dunleavy, Mike Newlin, Rick Barry and Calvin Murphy.

4. What was significant about the Detroit Pistons vs. Denver Nuggets game of Dec. 13, 1983?

Mike Dunleavy

It was the highest scoring game in history: Detroit 186, Denver 184.

5. What was significant about the Ft. Wayne Pistons vs. Minneapolis Lakers game of Nov. 22, 1950?

It was the lowest scoring game in history: Ft. Wayne 19, Minneapolis 18.

6. In that low scoring game, how many points were scored by Lakers other than George Mikan?

Three.

7. When did the National Basketball Association have its inaugural season?

1946-47.

8. What two leagues merged to form the NBA?

Basketball Association of America and National Basketball League.

9. What team won the championship in that inaugural season?

Philadelphia Warriors.

10. What team did the Warriors beat in the championship series of that inaugural season?

Chicago Stags.

11. When did the Chicago Bulls win their first NBA championship?

1991.

12. Over the course of that 1990-91 season, how many players actually played for the Bulls?

Twelve.

13. Name those 12 Bulls.

Michael Jordan, Scottie Pippen, Horace Grant, Bill Cartwright, B.J. Armstrong, John Paxson, Stacey King, Craig Hodges, Dennis Hopson, Will Perdue, Cliff Levingston and Scott Williams.

14. What two teams share the record for losing 23 games in a row in one season?

Denver (1997-98) and Vancouver (1995-96).

Scottie Pippen

15. What team set the record by winning 81.6 percent of its road games in 1971-72?

Los Angeles Lakers.

16. True or False. There never has been an NBA Final game in Indianapolis.

False. The Ft. Wayne Pistons played three games in Indianapolis in the 1955 Final because their home arena was being used for a professional bowling tournament.

17. What was the first NBA team to play a series of exhibition games in the Soviet Union?

Atlanta Hawks in 1988.

18. What team hosted the first McDonalds Open in 1987 featuring foreign championship teams?

Milwaukee Bucks.

19. What were the Philadelphia 76ers known as when they were located in Syracuse?

Syracuse Nationals.

20. What are the only two of the original 11 NBA franchises that have not moved or disbanded?

Boston Celtics and New York Knicks.

21. What was the worst record for any team that qualified for the playoffs?

16-54 (.229) by the Baltimore Bullets in 1952-53.

22. In the 1980s, the Los Angeles Lakers won nine Pacific Division titles. What team did they finish second to in 1980-81?

Phoenix Suns.

23. Neither Phoenix nor the Lakers won the Western Conference finals in 1981. What team did?

Houston Rockets.

24. What is the only team to miss the NBA playoffs a year after winning the championship?

1969-70 Boston Celtics.

25. The NBA's Most Valuable Player award is named The Maurice Podoloff Trophy. Why?

Podoloff was the first commissioner of the NBA.

26. How many of the 10 teams had winning records in 1966-67?

Three.

27. What was the last team to have six players score 1,000 or more points?

1990-91 Boston Celtics (Lewis, Gamble, McHale, Parish, Bird and Shaw).

28. What was the first team to win the NBA title without having a home court advantage in any playoff round?

The 1968-69 Boston Celtics.

29. What NBA team preceded the Raptors in Toronto by 49 years?

The Huskies.

30. What NBA team's uniforms had a silhouette of a bridge and the words "The City?"

San Francisco Warriors.

31. What is the only NBA team to have fuschia as one of its team colors?

San Antonio.

32. What expansion team has won the most games in its inaugural season?

1966-67 Chicago Bulls (33 wins).

33. Why is uniform No. 6 retired by the Sacramento Kings?

To honor their fans, the Sixth Man.

34. What are the three smallest cities ever to have an NBA franchise?

Anderson, Indiana (Packers), Sheboygan, Wisconsin (Redskins) and Waterloo, Iowa (Hawks).

35. What is the smallest city to have an NBA franchise today?

Salt Lake City.

36. What is the best overall winning percentage by an NBA franchise?

.612 by the Chicago Stags, 1946-50.

37. What is the second best overall winning percentage by an NBA franchise?

.611 by the Minneapolis/Los Angeles Lakers.

Match these defunct NBA teams with their home cities:

38. Stags	a. Waterloo
39. Rebels	b. Pittsburgh
40. Falcons	c. Chicago
41. Jets	d. Cincinnati
42. Nationals	e. Indianapolis
43. Ironmen	f. Washington
44. Royals	g. St. Louis
45. Bombers	h. Cleveland
46. Capitols	i. Syracuse
47. Hawks	j. Detroit

38. c, 39. h, 40. j, 41. e, 42. i, 43. b, 44. d, 45. g, 46. f, 47. a.

NBA PLAYERS

48. How many times did Jerry West lead the NBA in scoring?

Once, in 1969-70.

49. How many times did Elgin Baylor lead the NBA in scoring?

None.

50. How many times did Julius Erving lead the NBA in scoring?

None.

51. Who was the two-handed jump-shooter to lead the NBA in scoring in the inaugural season of 1946-47?

Joe Fulks.

52. Who is the only Boston Celtic to lead the NBA in scoring?

No one from Boston has won the title.

53. What franchise has had the most league scoring champions?

Philadelphia/Golden State Warriors with 12.

Elgin Baylor

54. Who is widely regarded as the last of the two-handed set shooters in the NBA?

Larry Costello.

55. Who is the only player to lead the league in scoring and assists in the same season?

Nate "Tiny" Archibald of Kansas City-Omaha in 1972-73.

56. Who holds the record for most career points in the playoffs?

Michael Jordan.

57. What team did Jerry Sloan play for in his rookie season?

Baltimore Bullets.

58. Who did the Associated Press name as the Player of the First Half Century?

George Mikan.

59. The NBA picked 25th, 35th and 50th anniversary all-time teams. Who are the only four players to make all three squads?

George Mikan, Bill Russell, Bob Pettit and Bob Cousy.

Julius Erving

Michael Jordan

60. Christian Laettner was traded with Sean Rooks from the Minnesota Timberwolves to the Atlanta Hawks for what two players?

Spud Webb and Andrew Lang.

61. True or False? Michael Jordan failed to hit above the "Mendoza Line" in his one season of minor league baseball.

False, but barely. He hit .202.

62. True or False? Michael Jordan never has led the NBA in field goal percentage for a season.

True.

63. Who is the only player to lead the league in field goal and free throw percentages in the same season?

Bob Feerick.

64. Who was the only one of the NBA's 50 Greatest Players who is no longer living?

Pete Maravich.

65. Who is the only NBA player born in the Virgin Islands?

Tim Duncan.

Steve Kerr

66. Who is the only NBA player from the island republic of the Grenadines?

Adonal Foyle.

67. Name two NBA players born in Lebanon.

Rony Seikaly and Steve Kerr.

Kevin McHale

68. Name two former NBA players born in Panama.

Rolando Blackman and Stuart Gray.

69. What former NBA all-star went to the same high school as singer Bob Dylan?

Kevin McHale in Hibbing, Minnesota.

70. Who are the four players to have uniform numbers retired by the Golden State Warriors?

Tom Meschery (No. 14), Al Attles (16), Rick Barry (24) and Nate Thurmond (42).

71. Name the five players who all averaged more than 30 points a game in 1961-62.

Wilt Chamberlain, Walt Bellamy, Bob Pettit, Oscar Robertson and Jerry West.

72. Who is the only player to lead the NBA in scoring and rebounding in the same season?

Wilt Chamberlain, five times.

73. Who are the only brothers to earn first-team All-Rookie in the same season?

Tom and Dick VanArsdale.

74. With what team did Rick Barry finish his NBA career?

Houston Rockets in 1980.

75. Who holds the NBA record by making 8,531 free throws in his career?

Moses Malone.

76. Who is the only player to record more than 2,000 rebounds in a season?

Wilt Chamberlain, twice, 1960-61 and 1961-62.

Charles Barkley

77. Who is the shortest player to win the NBA rebounding title?

Charles Barkley at 6-foot-6.

78. Who is the only center to lead the league in assists?

Wilt Chamberlain.

79. Only three players have had more than 1,000 assists in a season. Name them.

John Stockton, Isiah Thomas and Kevin Porter.

80. How many consecutive seasons did John Stockton lead the NBA in assists?

Nine, from 1987-88 through 1995-96.

81. Who holds the record for most blocked shots in a game?

Elmore Smith, 17.

82. Caldwell Jones had three brothers play in the NBA. Name them.

Charles, Major and Wilbert.

83. Who are the only two players to win the All-Star, Regular Season and NBA Finals MVP in the same season?

Michael Jordan and Willis Reed.

Isaiah Thomas

84. Who holds the record for most points in Game 7 of the NBA Finals?

Jerry West, 42 points in 1969.

85. What two players share the record for most assists in a playoff game?

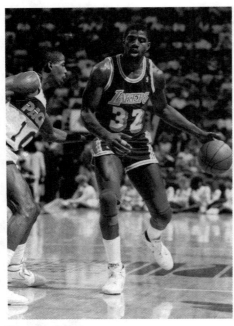

Magic Johnson

Magic Johnson and John Stockton.

86. Who is the youngest player to start an NBA All-Star game?

Kobe Bryant.

87. Who is the only player to win back-to-back MVPs with two different teams?

Moses Malone with Houston and Philadelphia.

88. Who is only player to win back-to-back NBA titles with two different teams?

Dennis Rodman.

89. Name any of the five players who were teammates of both Wilt Chamberlain and Bill Russell.

Woody Sauldsberry, Gary Phillips, Gary Ward, Willie Naulls and Mel Counts.

90. Who was the only player to be a teammate of Larry Bird and Magic Johnson?

Andre Turner.

91. Of players who have played at least two years, only one has more fouls than points in his career. Who is he?

Charles Jones had 2,079 fouls and 1,826 points in 15 NBA seasons.

92. John Starks attended four colleges. Name one of them.

Northern Oklahoma College, Rogers State (Oklahoma), Oklahoma Jr. College and Oklahoma State University.

93. Bill Russell won the NBA MVP award five times. How many times was he chosen to the 1st team All-NBA squad?

Three times.

94. Prior to Michael Jordan, who was the last player to lead the league in scoring while playing on the championship team?

Kareem Abdul-Jabbar, 1970-71.

95. Who was the only NBA Finals MVP from the losing team?

Jerry West in 1969.

96. What NBA player is a cousin of Denver Broncos defensive end Marvin Washington?

Andrew Lang.

97. Who is the only Nigerian to be named the NBA's Defensive Player of the Year?

Hakeem Olajuwon.

Kareem Abdul-Jabbar

98. What 5-foot-7 leaper won the 1986 Slam Dunk championship?

Spud Webb.

99. In his 12-year NBA career, Spud Webb has led the league in what statistical category?

Free throw percentage in 1994-95.

100. Who set the NBA record with 30 assists in a game?

Scott Skiles.

101. Who holds the NBA career record for steals?

John Stockton.

102. Who set the NBA season record with 301 steals?

Alvin Robertson.

Scott Skiles

103. More than a dozen players have recorded 10 steals in a game, but who is the only player to register a record 11 thefts?

Larry Kenon.

Alvin Robertson

104. Besides Kareem Abdul-Jabbar, who is the only player to lead the NBA in blocked shots in a season four times?

Mark Eaton.

105. Blocked shots became a yearly statistical category in 1973-74. Who was the first league leader?

Elmore Smith.

106. Who was the first NBA player to score 20,000 points?

Bob Pettit.

107. Who played two seasons in the NBA and was a member of the Lakers' 1950 championship team, yet is more remembered for coaching an NFL team to four Super Bowls?

Bud Grant.

108. Before Michael Jordan, who was the only player to lead the NBA scoring the same year his team won the NBA championship?

Kareem Abdul-Jabbar.

109. Name one of the two players who share the NBA record by making 28 free throws in a game.

Adrian Dantley and Wilt Chamberlain.

110. True or False. Billy Knight is one of just 10 NBA players to score more than 2,000 points in his rookie season.

True.

111. Since Wilt Chamberlain set the NBA rookie record with 58 points in a game, who has scored the next highest total as a first-year player?

Billy Knight

Rick Barry, 57 points.

112. Who are the only three players to score more than 20,000 career points without averaging at least 20 points a game?

Robert Parish, Hal Greer and Tom Chambers.

113. Who never averaged more than 11 points a game in his 11-year career and never made an all-star team, yet had his uniform No. 16 retired by the Warriors?

Al Attles.

114. Who averaged just 7.4 points a game in his nine-year career and never made an all-star team, yet had his uniform No. 25 retired by the Celtics?

K.C. Jones.

115. Who is the only Dallas Maverick to have his uniform number retired? Hint: He wore No. 15.

Brad Davis.

116. What uniform number did George Mikan wear?

No. 99.

Brad Davis

117. Several players have had their uniform number retired by two teams, but only two players had two different numbers retired by the two teams. Who are they?

Oscar Robertson; No. 1 at Milwaukee and No. 14 at Cincinnati; and Julius Erving (No. 32 with New Jersey and No. 6 with Philadelphia).

118. Who grabbed 38 percent of his team's total rebounds in 1978-79, the highest percentage ever?

Moses Malone.

119. Who was the back-up center behind Wilt Chamberlain in 1961-62 when he averaged 48.5 minutes a game?

Joe Ruklick.

120. What Rhodes Scholar spent two years at Oxford before joining the Knicks?

Bill Bradley.

121. In the 1960s, who was the Knicks' starting center, forcing Willis Reed to play power-forward in his first three seasons?

Walt Bellamy.

122. Where did Elvin Hayes play his first three pro seasons?

With the San Diego Rockets.

123. What future Hall of Famer tied for first in the high jump at the 1957 Drake Relays?

Wilt Chamberlain.

124. In 1970-71 and 1994-95, the NBA Rookie of the Year awards were shared. Name the pairs.

Dave Cowens and Geoff Petrie; Grant Hill and Jason Kidd.

125. Who briefly toyed with dunking his free throws until the rules makers rejected the notion?

Wilt Chamberlain.

126. Who is the only NBA player ever caught fixing games?

Jack Molinas.

127. Who was the first NBA player to score 2,000 points in a season?

George Yardley.

128. Who was the first player to record a quadruple-double?

Nate Thurmond.

129. Only three other players have achieved a quadruple-double since Nate Thurmond. Who are they?

Alvin Robertson, Hakeem Olajuwon and David Robinson.

130. Who is the only player to lead the NCAA, NBA and ABA in scoring?

Rick Barry.

131. Prior to 1985, how many times had a guard been chosen league MVP?

Twice, Bob Cousy and Oscar Robertson.

132. Who is the only Cleveland Cavalier to start in the All-Star Game? Hint: It happened in 1998.

Shawn Kemp.

133. Who is the youngest player in NBA history?

Jermaine O'Neal of Portland.

134. In the summer of 1966, the 76ers signed Wilt Chamberlain to a contract worth $100,000. How much did Bill Russell sign for later that summer?

$100,001.

135. In 1966-67, who broke Wilt Chamberlain's streak of leading the league in scoring seven straight years?

Dave Bing.

136. After playing 11 seasons on different teams, what NBA team reunited twins Dick and Tom Van Arsdale?

Phoenix Suns.

137. Who was the former NBA all-star that played professionally in Israel at the age of 36?

Tom Chambers.

138. True or False? Wilt Chamberlain led the NBA in assists in 1967-68?

True.

Tom Chambers

139. True or False? Wilt Chamberlain never fouled out of any of his 1,045 games in the NBA.

True.

140. What's the quickest anyone has fouled out of an NBA game?

Three minutes by Bubba Wells.

141. Who holds the record for most consecutive free throws made?

Micheal Williams, 97.

142. Who are the two players from Washington, D.C.'s, Spingarn High School that are in the Hall of Fame today?

Elgin Baylor and Dave Bing.

143. Who is the son of a Baptist preacher that changed his first name to Jamaal when he became a Muslim?

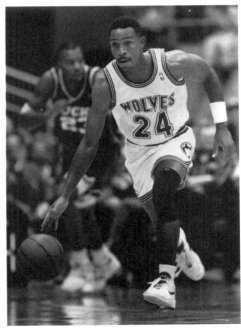

Micheal Williams

Keith Wilkes.

144. What NBA player is married to Debbie Allen of the television show *Fame*?

Norm Nixon.

145. What NBA player suffers from Tourette's Syndrome?

Mahmoud Abdul-Rauf.

146. How many years did David Robinson serve in the Navy between the end of his academy career and his first game with the San Antonio Spurs?

Two.

Norm Nixon

147. Who made the first three-point field goal in an NBA game?

Chris Ford of the Celtics.

148. What tough-guy was thrown out of a record 127 games?

Vern Mikkelson.

149. Who holds the single-season record for highest free throw percentage?

Calvin Murphy, .958 in 1980-81.

150. In what other athletic endeavor did Calvin Murphy earn national acclaim?

Baton twirling.

151. Who is the most accurate underhanded free throw shooter in NBA history?

Rick Barry.

152. Tyrone Corbin played for eight different NBA teams in his 13-year career. Name two of them.

San Antonio, Cleveland, Phoenix, Minnesota, Utah, Atlanta, Miami and Sacramento.

153. Who was the player that played with five different teams in the 1992-93 season?

Alex Stivrins.

Match these NBA players with their alma maters:

154. Sleepy Floyd	a. Southern Illinois
155. Popeye Jones	b. Murray State
156. Alex English	c. Georgetown
157. Walt Frazier	d. Clemson
158. Bob Sura	e. Syracuse
159. Kerry Kittles	f. Utah
160. Billy Owens	g. South Carolina
161. Keith Van Horn	h. Kansas
162. JoJo White	i. Florida State
163. Elden Campbell	j. Villanova

154. c, 155. b, 156. g, 157. a, 158. i, 159. j, 160. e, 161. f, 162. h, 163. d.

164. Which NBA player is known as "The Mayor?"

Fred Hoiberg.

165. Who was known as "The Pearl?"

Earl Monroe.

166. Who was known as "The Microwave?"

Vinnie Johnson.

167. Who was known as "Cornbread?"

Cedric Maxwell.

168. Cedric Maxwell nicknamed Robert Parish "Chief" because of what popular movie?

One Flew Over the Cuckoo's Nest.

169. Who was known as "Zeke from Cabin Creek?"

Jerry West.

170. What two players shared the nickname "The Dream?"

Hakeem Olajuwon and Dean Meminger.

171. What is Muggsy Bogues's first name?

Tyrone.

172. What is Cherokee Parks's first name?

Cherokee.

Muggsy Bogues

173. What is Terry Dehere's full name?

Lennox Dominique Dehere.

174. What is Chris Webber's full name?

Mayce Edward Christopher Webber III.

175. From A to Z, what player has the most As and Zs in his name?

Zaid Abdul-Aziz, who used to be called Don Smith.

176. What NBA all-star doubled as his college team's student manager?

Scottie Pippen.

177. What Hall of Famer wrote a book that has sold more than 2 million copies?

Jerry Lucas.

178. Where was Larry Bird's last official appearance as a player?

Barcelona, Spain, in the 1992 Olympics.

179. Who held the NBA's single-game scoring record for only one year before it was broken by Wilt Chamberlain?

Elgin Baylor.

Larry Bird

180. Wilt Chamberlain averaged 22.9 rebounds a game in his career. How many rebounds did he average per game in his 142 head-to-head matches with Bill Russell?

28.7.

181. How many rebounds a game did Bill Russell average in his head-to-head competition with Wilt Chamberlain?

23.7.

182. In Wilt Chamberlain's final head-to-head match-up with Kareem Abdul-Jabbar, how many points did they each have?

Abdul-Jabbar scored 24, Chamberlain 0.

183. When Walt Bellamy played in an NBA-record 88 games in a season in 1968-69, what two teams did he play with?

New York and Detroit.

184. What former NBA player now makes a living playing the bass and recording jazz albums?

Wayman Tisdale.

185. Who is the only former Texas high schooler to play for the Dallas Mavericks?

Reggie Slater.

186. Who had the most points in any game in the 1970s?

David Thompson, 73.

187. Who had the most points in any game in the 1980s?

Wayman Tisdale

Michael Jordan, 61 (twice).

188. Who had the most points in any game in the 1990s?

Michael Jordan, 69.

189. What former Big Ten All-American now is in charge of basketball operations for his home state team?

Kevin McHale.

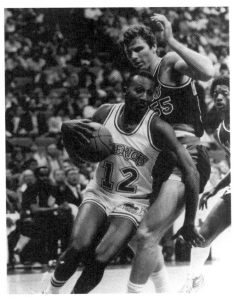

190. Who is the only NBA player that increased his scoring average in each of his first eight seasons?

Derek Harper.

191. Who is the only player to record a triple-double in an All-Star game?

Derek Harper

Michael Jordan.

192. What player averaged 31.6 points a game as a rookie, then saw his average drop every season for six straight years?

Walt Bellamy.

193. What two players were members of both the 1971-72 Lakers (69-13) and 1972-73 Philadelphia 76ers (9-73)?

LeRoy Ellis and John Q. Trapp.

194. What Hall of Fame basketball player was drafted by the Cleveland Browns of the National Football League?

John Havlicek.

195. Who is the oldest player to win the MVP award?

Michael Jordan.

196. What power forward is credited with bagging the seventh largest mountain lion in the world?

Karl Malone.

197. Who was the first African-American drafted by an NBA team?

Chuck Cooper.

198. Who was the first African-American signed by an NBA team?

Nat "Sweetwater" Clifton.

199. Who was the first African-American to play in an NBA game?

Earl Lloyd.

200. Who were the first two African-Americans to play on a championship team?

Jim Tucker and Earl Lloyd.

201. Before all of that, though, the Rochester Royals of the National Basketball League had two African-American players in 1946. Name them.

Pop Gates and Dolly King.

202. What Caucasian scored the most points in an NBA game?

Pete Maravich.

203. Who is the only Caucasian to win the NBA Slam Dunk title?

Brent Barry.

204. What NBA player was chosen to play in a record 19 all-star games?

Kareem Abdul-Jabbar.

205. Who is the only player to win championships in the NCAA, NBA and ABA?

Tom Thacker.

206. Who won the NBA Rookie of the Year award in Jerry West's rookie season?

Oscar Robertson.

207. Name the four Celtics who have been named the NBA MVP.

Bill Russell (4 times), Larry Bird (3), Bob Cousy (1) and Dave Cowens (1).

208. Who was the winner of the first Sixth Man of the Year award in 1982-83?

Bobby Jones.

Eddie Johnson

209. Who are the two Phoenix Suns who won the Sixth Man of the Year award?

Danny Manning and Eddie Johnson.

210. Who earned the Sixth Man of the Year award twice while a member of the Milwaukee Bucks?

Ricky Pierce.

211. What former Kentucky star was the first of Boston's famed Sixth Man?

Frank Ramsey.

212. Who are the only three players to average 20 points and 20 rebounds in a season?

Ricky Pierce

Wilt Chamberlain, Bob Pettit and Jerry Lucas.

213. Who is the only player to average a triple-double for an entire season?

Oscar Robertson.

214. Karl Malone finished third in the balloting for Rookie of the Year in 1985-86. Who were the two players who finished ahead of him?

Patrick Ewing and Xavier McDaniel.

Dominique Wilkins

215. The year before Michael Jordan won his first NBA scoring title, who was the league's top scorer?

Dominique Wilkins.

216. Who is the last left-handed player to lead the NBA in free throw percentage?

Chris Mullin.

217. When was the last time teammates scored 2,000 points in the same season? Who were the players?

1986-87 Boston Celtics; Larry Bird and Kevin McHale.

Chris Mullin

218. Who is Hartford University's only pro player ever?

Vin Baker.

219. When the last time two rookies from the same team played in the All-Star game and who were they?

1982, Detroit's Isiah Thomas and Kelly Tripucka.

220. When A.C. Green broke the NBA record for consecutive games played, whose record did he break?

Randy Smith.

Vin Baker

221. Who has made the most career 3-pointers in NBA history?

Reggie Miller.

222. Who has the highest career field goal percentage in the playoffs (minimum 150 made)?

James Donaldson.

James Donaldson

223. Prior to 1997-98, no NBA team had ever had more than two players with more than 1,000 games of experience. Name the team and players in 1997-98 that had a record five players with more than 1,000 games.

Houston Rockets; Charles Barkley, Clyde Drexler, Eddie Johnson, Hakeem Olajuwon and Kevin Willis.

224. When Detroit traded Bob Lanier to Milwaukee in 1980, what did the Pistons get in return?

Kent Benson and a first-round draft choice.

225. Gus Williams received the Comeback Player of the Year award in 1981-82. Why had he missed the 1980-81 season?

He sat out the season in a contract dispute.

226. Who won the Most Improved Player award in 1991-92 after nearly doubling his scoring average to 20 points a game?

Pervis Ellison.

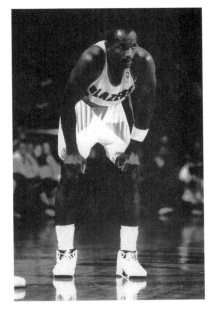

Clyde Drexler

227. Name the two foreign-born players who have won the Most Improved Player award?

Rony Seikaly and Gheorghe Muresan.

Pervis Ellison

228. Who are the only two rookies to win the NBA Most Valuable Player award?

Wilt Chamberlain and Wes Unseld.

229. Who are the only two players to win the Rookie of the Year and MVP award in successive seasons?

Bob Pettit and Kareem Abdul-Jabbar.

230. Who was the first player to enter the NBA prior to his college class's graduation to earn Rookie of the Year honors?

Alvin Adams in 1976.

231. Who are the two NBA players who played at Rindge & Latin High School in Cambridge, Massachusetts?

Patrick Ewing and Rumeal Robinson.

232. Who are the only four players on the NBA's top 10 career lists for points and rebounds?

Kareem Abdul-Jabbar, Wilt Chamberlain, Moses Malone and Elvin Hayes.

Alvin Adams

233. Who is the only player who ranks on the NBA's top 10 career list for points and assists?

Oscar Robertson.

234. What lefty holds the NBA career record for field goal percentage?

Artis Gilmore.

235. Who wound up his career with exactly 50,000 minutes played?

Elvin Hayes.

236. Bob Cousy led the NBA in assists for eight straight seasons. Who snapped his streak in 1960-61?

Oscar Robertson.

237. Before Oscar Robertson and Jerry West entered the league, with guard had the highest scoring average for a season?

Gene Shue, 22.8 points per game.

238. Who was the last Knick to lead the league in assists?

Michael Ray Richardson.

239. Who was the first Knick to lead the league in scoring?

Bernard King.

240. Who is the only Buffalo Brave to lead the league in scoring?

Bob McAdoo.

241. Who is the only Utah Jazz player to lead the league in scoring?

Gene Shue

Adrian Dantley.

242. Who was the Lakers' center from Iceland?

Petur Gudmundsson.

243. Who did Denver receive in a trade with Philadelphia in 1978 in exchange for Bobby Jones and Ralph Simpson?

George McGinnis.

244. Of the 10 greatest single-game scoring marks, how many belong to Michael Jordan?

One.

245. Of the 10 greatest single-game scoring marks, how many belong to Wilt Chamberlain?

Six.

246. What SuperSonic played a record 69 minutes in a game in 1989?

Dale Ellis.

247. Kareem Abdul-Jabbar holds the record with 19 1,000-point seasons. Who is second with 16?

John Havlicek.

248. What U. of New Mexico alum was regarded as the best defensive player of the 1980s, even though he won only one Defensive Player of the Year award?

Michael Cooper.

George McGinnis

249. Who won two Defensive Player of the Year awards in the Big East, then added three more awards in the NBA in the 1990s?

Dikembe Mutombo.

Michael Cooper

250. What is Dikembe Mutombo's full name?

Dikembe Mutombo Mpolondo Mukamba Jean Jacque Wamutombo.

251. What do the initials T.R. in T.R. Dunn stand for?

Theodore Roosevelt.

252. What team did Walt Frazier finish his playing career with?

Cleveland Cavaliers.

253. In his career, Wilt Chamberlain was traded twice for a total of six players. Name any of them.

Paul Neumann, Connie Dierking, Lee Shaffer, Jerry Chambers, Archie Clark and Darrall Imhoff.

254. Who was the first player ever ejected from an NBA game?

Ed Sadowski in 1946.

NBA Coaches

Q.

255. After the Minneapolis Lakers moved to Los Angeles, their coach, John Kundla, remained in Minnesota in what capacity?

As coach of the University of Minnesota basketball team.

256. What NBA coach won 500 games the fastest?

Phil Jackson in 682 games.

257. What coach got to 500 wins the second fastest?

Pat Riley in 684 games.

Pat Riley

258. Jack Ramsay was the head coach at Portland from 1976-86. Who were the head coaches at Portland before and after Ramsay?

Lenny Wilkens and Mike Schuler.

259. Chuck Daly was the head coach at Detroit from 1983-92. Who were the head coaches at Detroit before and after Daly?

Scotty Robertson and Ron Rothstein.

Jack Ramsay

Chuck Daly

260. Name either of the two Continental Basketball Association teams coached by George Karl.

Montana and Albany.

261. Who guided Grand Canyon College to the 1988 NAIA championship?

Paul Westphal.

262. Danny Ainge played four seasons of professional baseball for what organization?

Toronto Blue Jays.

George Karl

263. How many different NBA teams did Bill Fitch coach?

Five; Cleveland, Boston, Houston, New Jersey and the Los Angeles Clippers.

Danny Ainge

Cotton Fitzsimmons

264. The Minnesota Timberwolves have had five head coaches in their history. Name two of them.

Bill Musselman, Jimmy Rodgers, Sidney Lowe, Bill Blair and Flip Saunders.

265. What is Red Auerbach's first name?

Arnold.

266. Who cut former baseball commissioner Bowie Kuhn from his high school basketball team?

Red Auerbach.

267. What NBA coach graduated from Aviation High School in Redondo Beach, California?

Paul Westphal.

268. What is Cotton Fitzsimmons' first name?

Lowell.

269. Name Butch Carter's famous brother.

NFL wide receiver Cris Carter.

270. Who was the first African-American named head coach in the Boston?

Bill Russell.

271. Who was the first person to coach two different NBA teams in the same season?

Larry Brown.

272. Two years after he retired from the Boston Celtics, Dave Cowens returned to play 40 games for what team?

Milwaukee Bucks.

273. Who was the head coach of the 1967 NBA championship team and the 1969 ABA championship team?

Alex Hannum.

274. Who is the only coach to win NBA titles with two different franchises?

Alex Hannum; 1958 St. Louis and 1967 Philadelphia.

Bill Sharman

275. Who is the only coach to win a title in the NBA, ABA and ABL?

Bill Sharman.

276. What future NBA coach is the only player in Major League Baseball history to get thrown out of a game without ever actually playing a big league game in his career?

Bill Sharman. He was a late-season call-up and got tossed out of the final game of the season when he and his teammates were razzing the umpires from the dugout. He never got another opportunity in the bigs.

277. Who is the only person to win Coach of the Year and Executive of the Year in the same season?

Frank Layden in 1983-84.

Frank Layden

278. The Celtics won 11 of 13 titles from 1957-69. Who was the coach that won both of the "other" championships?

Alex Hannum.

279. What NBA mentor coached 10 games as a 24-year-old in the All-American Basketball Association in 1977-78?

Mike Dunleavy.

280. Who was the first coach of the New York Knicks?

Neil Cohalan.

281. Who is the only three-time winner of the Coach of the Year award?

Pat Riley.

282. From 1990-98, only one winner of the Coach of the Year award was not a former NBA player. Who was he?

Del Harris.

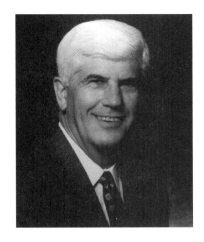

Del Harris

283. What NBA coach also managed in the Major Leagues?

Red Rolfe coached the Toronto Huskies and managed the Detroit Tigers.

Red Auerbach

284. Who is the NBA Coach of the Year award named in honor of?

Red Auerbach.

285. Who are the only four coaches to win the Coach of the Year award the same year that they won the NBA title?

Bill Sharman, Red Holzman, Red Auerbach and Phil Jackson.

286. Who are the only two coaches to lose more than 1,000 NBA games?

Bill Fitch

Bill Fitch and Dick Motta.

287. Who replaced both Kevin Loughery in Miami and Doug Collins in Detroit as interim head coach?

Alvin Gentry.

288. Who replaced both Hubie Brown in New York and Dick Versace in Indiana as interim head coach?

Bob Hill.

289. Who is the only person to win the Coach of the Year award and the MVP trophy?

Larry Bird.

290. Who are the only two coaches to win the Rookie of the Year and Coach of the Year awards?

Tom Heinsohn and Larry Bird.

291. Besides Larry Bird, what other (former) NBA head coach grew up in French Lick, Indiana?

Jerry Reynolds.

292. Who coached the Lakers to the NBA Final, the Colonels to the ABA Final and Providence to two NIT championships?

Joe Mullaney.

293. Who is the only coach to win titles in three different divisions?

Bill Fitch.

294. Who are the only three men who played in the NCAA title game and also coached an NBA championship team?

K.C. Jones, Bill Russell and Pat Riley.

295. What NBA coach played 14 years for three teams and is remembered for shooting his free throws with one hand?

Don Nelson.

296. What NBA coach's father was a member of the first NBA championship team?

Matt Goukas.

Don Nelson

Lenny Wilkens

297. The J. Walter Kennedy Citizenship award has been presented to 24 players and one coach. Who was the good guy coach?

Frank Layden.

298. What number did the Knicks retire in honor of Red Holzman?

No. 613 (the number of games he won as a Knicks coach).

299. Who holds the record for most NBA wins?

Lenny Wilkens.

300. Who is the only active NBA coach whose brother also was an NBA head coach?

Larry Brown and his brother, Herb.

Larry Brown

301. Who is the only coach to record 60-win seasons for three different franchises?

Pat Riley for the Lakers, Knicks and Heat.

302. What former NBA coach's mother wrote the book which became the basis of the TV show *The Flying Nun*?

Dick Versace; his mother is Tere Rios.

303. Name the four future NBA coaches who were members of the 1964-65 Boston Celtics.

Bill Russell, K.C. Jones, Tom Heinsohn and Tom Sanders.

K.C. Jones

304. Name any of the four NBA coaches in the Naismith Basketball Hall of Fame who did not win an NBA championship.

Alvin Julian, Harry Litwack, Kenneth Loeffler and Frank McGuire.

305. So far, who is the only NBA referee who became an NBA coach?

Charley Eckman.

306. What future NBA coach was the second leading scorer behind Wilt Chamberlain the night Chamberlain scored 100 points?

Al Attles.

307. Bob Cousy's only NBA coaching experience was with what team?

Cincinnati Royals.

308. Who was the first coach of the Boston Celtics? Red Auerbach, Alvin Julian or John Russell?

John Russell.

Bob Cousy

309. Where was Paul Westphal an All-American college player?

University of Southern California.

310. Where did former coach turned announcer Hubie Brown play in college?

Niagara.

Paul Westphal

311. Who was Hubie Brown's college teammate who also became an NBA head coach?

Frank Layden.

312. What former NBA coach served as the commissioner of the American Soccer League from 1975-80?

Bob Cousy.

NBA DRAFT

313. Which of these players was not a No. 1 overall pick? Pervis Ellison, Harold Miner or LaRue Martin?

Harold Miner.

314. How many more college seasons did Larry Bird play after being drafted by the Boston Celtics?

One.

315. How many more college seasons did Bob McAdoo play after being drafted by the Buffalo Braves?

None.

316. Who is the only person selected in the first round of the NBA and Major League Baseball drafts?

Scott Burrell, by the Charlotte Hornets and Toronto Blue Jays.

317. Prior to Allen Iverson in 1996, who was the last guard chosen No. 1 overall in the NBA draft?

Magic Johnson.

318. When the Lakers selected Magic Johnson with the No. 1 pick, from what team did the Lakers receive that selection?

New Orleans Jazz.

319. What NBA team drafted Dave Winfield?

Atlanta Hawks, 5th round in 1973.

320. What team drafted Bill Russell?

St. Louis Hawks.

321. What team chose Oscar Robertson as a "Territorial Draft Selection"?

Cincinnati Royals.

322. Spencer Haywood was drafted (but not signed) by what NBA team?

Buffalo Braves.

323. Who did the Baltimore Bullets select in the first-round of the 1971 draft, even though doing so caused them to forfeit their 1972 first round pick?

Phil Chenier.

324. From 1966-84, the NBA used a coin flip between conference doormats to see which would select first in the draft. How many times in the those 19 flips did the coin come up heads?

Seven.

325. What team lost the coin flip prior to the 1969 draft (which allowed Milwaukee to take Lew Alcindor)?

Phoenix Suns.

Terry Cummings

326. Who did Phoenix take with the second pick in 1969?

Neal Walk.

327. Who is the last Rookie of the Year who wasn't selected in the first round?

Willis Reed in 1964-65.

328. What do Tom Chambers, Terry Cummings, Adrian Dantley, Byron Scott, Hersey Hawkins and Danny Manning have in common?

They all were first-round selections of the Los Angeles Clippers.

329. In 1998 Dallas drafted Ansu Sesay. What country is Sesay from?

U.S.A.

330. Cleveland selected Campy Russell (no relation to Cazzie) in the first round of the 1974 draft. Who was Campy named in honor of?

Roy Campanella.

331. Who was the only first-round NBA draft pick in 1967 who signed with an ABA team?

Mel Daniels.

Mel Daniels

332. Who was drafted by Phoenix in 1988, but did not play in the NBA until 1996 with Minnesota?

Dean Garrett.

333. In the 1984 draft, Houston used the No. 1 pick on Akeem Olajuwon and Chicago used the No. 3 pick on Michael Jordan. Who did Portland select with the No. 2 pick?

Sam Bowie.

334. Besides Sam Bowie, what Kentucky star also was selected in the first round of the 1984 draft?

Mel Turpin.

335. Bill Russell was just the second player chosen in the 1956 draft. Who went No. 1?

Sihugo Green.

336. In 1981 the New Jersey Nets drafted Vic Sison from UCLA in the 10th round. Sison never played a minute at UCLA. Why was he drafted?

Sison was the student manager at UCLA under incoming Nets coach Larry Brown.

Patrick Ewing

337. Who was drafted in the first round of the 1986 draft, yet didn't make his NBA debut until nine years later?

Arvydas Sabonis.

338. The lottery was instituted in 1985, primarily to keep teams from "tanking" games at the end of the season. What player was chosen No. 1 in 1985?

Patrick Ewing.

339. Prior to selecting Patrick Ewing with the No. 1 pick, when was the last time the Knicks had the No. 1 selection and who did they take?

1966; Cazzie Russell.

340. Who was Houston's first-round pick in 1998 that played for his father at Valparaiso?

Bryce Drew.

341. What legendary Iowa girls high school basketball star was drafted by Golden State?

Denise Long.

342. The first overall pick in the 1973 draft was used by Philadelphia on what future NBA coach?

Doug Collins.

343. In 1992 the NBA took its college draft on the road after always being held in New York. Where was the 1992 draft held?

Portland.

344. The Territorial Draft was used only occasionally from 1956-65. Who did Boston claim in the 1956 draft?

Tom Heinsohn from Holy Cross.

345. What four players did Cincinnati draft with territorial picks?

Oscar Robertson, Jerry Lucas, Tom Thacker and George Wilson.

346. In 1963, the Knicks allowed Syracuse to move to Philadelphia under the condition that the Knicks, not Philadelphia, could pick who with a territorial selection?

Bill Bradley of Princeton.

347. Who were the Sacramento Kings' four first-round picks in 1990?

Lionel Simmons, Travis Mays, Duane Causwell and Anthony Bonner.

348. Name any of the Celtics' first-round picks between 1980 (Kevin McHale) and 1987 (Reggie Lewis).

Charles Bradley (1981), Darren Tillis (1982), Greg Kite (1983), Michael Young (1984), Sam Vincent (1985) and Len Bias (1986).

349. Who were the three former Proviso East (Ill.) High School teammates selected in the 1995 draft?

Michael Finley, Sherell Ford and Donnie Boyce.

NBA OWNERS

Q.

350. What was the first team to have its stocks traded on a national market?

Boston Celtics.

351. What New York Stock Exchange listed company owns the Seattle SuperSonics?

Ackerley Group.

352. What former governor of Kentucky once owned the Boston Celtics?

John Y. Brown.

353. What former NBA owner was married to Phyllis George?

John Y. Brown.

354. How much did the owners of the Phoenix Suns pay for an expansion team in 1968?

$2 million.

355. How much did Isiah Thomas pay for 9 percent of the expansion Toronto Raptors in 1995?

$11.25 million.

356. Who was the trucking magnate who sold the Minneapolis Lakers and bought the Washington Senators?

Bob Short.

357. What owner produced several major motion pictures, including *Love at First Bite*?

Melvin Simon.

358. Ted Arison of the Miami Heat made his vast fortune in what business?

Carnival Cruise Lines.

359. Red McCombs has owned all or part of three sports teams in two sports in three leagues. Name them.

San Antonio Spurs (ABA and NBA), Denver Nuggets (NBA) and Minnesota Vikings (NFL).

360. The founder of The National Lampoon once owned a piece of which franchise?

Philadelphia Warriors.

361. In 1949, the Indianapolis Olympians were sold to a group of four former Kentucky players. Name them.

Alex Groza, Ralph Beard, Wallace Jones and Cliff Barker.

362. What was the fate of the Olympians?

In 1951 the owners were implicated in a game-throwing scandal from their college days and by 1954 the team was bankrupt and disbanded.

363. In the first nine years they spent in the NBA, the then Philadelphia Warriors were coached by their owner. Who was he?

Eddie Gottlieb.

364. Name the two owners who have had uniform No. 1 retired in their honor.

Boston's Walter Brown and Portland's Larry Weinberg.

365. In 1978 two owners traded their entire franchises. What two teams were involved?

Buffalo Braves and Boston Celtics.

366. What all-pro bought a third of his team and became the general manager?

George Mikan of the Minneapolis Lakers.

367. What NBA owners developed The Mall of America, the largest mall in the U.S.?

Melvin Simon and his brother, Herbert Simon.

368. Who was the first African-American to be a managing general partner of an NBA team?

Peter Bynoe of the Denver Nuggets.

369. Who was the first Asian-American to own a professional basketball team?

Art Kim who owned the Anaheim Amigos (ABA) in 1967.

Match these owners with teams they have owned:

370. Franklin Mieuli   a. Portland
371. George Shinn   b. Denver
372. Jack Kent Cooke   c. Washington
373. Abe Pollin   d. Chicago
374. Harry Glickman   e. Golden State
375. Gulf & Western Corp.   f. Phoenix
376. Comsat Corp.   g. Philadelphia
377. Harold Katz   h. Charlotte
378. Lamar Hunt   i. L.A. Lakers
379. Andy Williams   j. New York

370. e, 371. h, 372. i, 373. c, 374. a, 375. j, 376. b, 377. g, 378. d, 379. f.

NBA ARENAS

Q.

380. Where was the largest crowd to see an NBA game?

Atlanta's Georgia Dome (62,046). Chicago vs. Atlanta

381. Where was the largest crowd to see an NBA playoff game?

Pontiac's Silverdome (41,732).

382. Where was the largest crowd to see an NBA all-star game?

Houston's Astrodome (44,735).

383. Name the six NBA arenas named after airlines.

Utah's Delta Center, Chicago's United Center, Phoenix's America West Arena, Miami's American Airlines Arena, New Jersey's Continental Airlines Arena and Toronto's Air Canada Centre.

384. Name the four NBA arenas named after financial institutions.

Philadelphia's First Union Center, Seattle's Key Arena, Boston's Fleet Center and the Lakers' Great Western Forum.

385. What NBA city has an arena named after an automobile manufacturer?

Vancouver, Bear Country at General Motors Place.

386. What NBA arena is named after the owner?

Cleveland's Gund Arena.

387. Where was the first NBA All-Star Game held in 1951?

Boston Garden.

388. Name any of the six cities that has hosted the Nets' home games?

Paramus, N.J., Commack, N.Y., West Hempstead, N.Y., Uniondale, N.Y., Piscatoway, N.J., and East Rutherford, N.J.

389. What is the name of the new arena in Los Angeles?

Staples Center.

Match these former NBA arenas to the location:

390.	Cobo Hall	a.	San Francisco
391.	The Omni	b.	San Antonio
392.	Veterans Memorial Coliseum	c.	Detroit
393.	Kemper Arena	d.	Atlanta
394.	Cow Palace	e.	Cleveland
395.	HemisFair Arena	f.	Phoenix
396.	Salt Palace	g.	Utah
397.	Richfield Coliseum	h.	Kansas City
398.	Market Square Arena	i.	Philadelphia
399.	Convention Hall	j.	Indiana

390. c, 391. d, 392. f, 393. h, 394. a, 395. b, 396. g, 397. e, 398. j, 399. i.

400. When Wilt Chamberlain of the Philadelphia Warriors scored 100 points against the New York Knicks, what non-NBA arena was the site of the game?

Hershey (Pennsylvania) Arena.

401. How many people saw that record-breaking performance?

4,124.

402. What was the oldest arena still in use for the 1998-99 season?

Los Angeles Sports Arena (opened in 1959).

403. What arena did the Celtics use as a second home from 1974-90?

Hartford (Connecticut) Civic Center.

COLLEGE TEAMS

Q.

404. What is the only school to win both the NCAA championship and NIT in the same year?

City College of New York in 1950.

405. What school, led by Bill Russell and K.C. Jones, won a then-record 60 consecutive games?

San Francisco.

406. What school snapped San Francisco's winning streak?

Illinois.

407. What school held the consecutive victory streak prior to San Francisco?

Peru State Teachers of Nebraska with 55 straight wins from 1921-26.

408. UCLA's 88-game winning streak was broken by what school?

Notre Dame.

409. In 1966, Texas Western won the NCAA title. What is that school known as today?

University of Texas-El Paso.

410. Artis Gilmore was the star of what school that advanced to the NCAA Final in 1971?

Jacksonville.

411. What school was the first NCAA champion to lose at least seven games?

Marquette in 1977.

412. What are the two most recent Ivy League schools to make the Final Four?

Penn in 1979 and Princeton in 1965.

413. What is the only Ivy League school to play in the NCAA Final?

Dartmouth in 1942 and 1944.

414. When Florida State lost the 1972 NCAA Final to UCLA, what conference was it in?

None. FSU was an independent until it joined the Atlantic Coast Conference in 1992.

415. In 1981 what two schools played in the last third place game of the NCAA championships?

Virginia and LSU.

416. Georgia Tech had three players average more than 20 points a game in 1989-90, the only Final Four team to do so. Name the players.

Dennis Scott, Brian Oliver and Kenny Anderson.

417. Since UCLA in 1967, what was the only national championship team to return its starting unit the following season?

Arkansas in 1994-95; it finished second to UCLA in the 1995 tournament.

418. In 1989, what two teams played in the highest scoring game in history, 181-150?

Loyola Marymount and U.S. International.

419. What school finished ninth in the Big Ten in 1940, then won the NCAA championship in 1941?

Wisconsin.

420. What team went 30-0 and won the 1964 NCAA title without a player over 6-foot-5?

UCLA.

421. What is the lowest seeded team to reach the Final Four?

LSU, with an 11 seed in 1986.

422. What is the only school to lead the nation in scoring and win the NCAA title in the same season?

Ohio State in 1959-60.

423. What Southeastern Conference school featured the "Ernie and Bernie Show" in the 1970s?

Tennessee.

424. What school's high-flying team was dubbed Phi Slamma Jamma?

Houston.

425. What was Illinois' 1942 team known as?

The Whiz Kids.

Kentucky teams have been given nicknames on several occasions. Match these seasons with the nicknames:

426. 1947-48   a. Rupp's Runts
427. 1957-58   b. The Fiddlin' Five
428. 1965-66   c. The Fabulous Five

426. c, 427. b, 428. a.

429. What is the worst one-season record in Division I history?

0-28 by Prairie View in 1991-92.

430. What is the only Pac-10 school to not (yet) make the Final Four?

Arizona State.

431. What Pac-10 school played in the NCAA title game in 1959 and 1960?

California.

432. Name the five schools that comprise the Philadelphia Big 5.

Penn, LaSalle, St. Joseph's, Villanova, Temple.

433. What is the nickname of the Northern Arizona men's team?

Lumberjacks.

434. What is the nickname of the Northern Arizona women's team?

Lumberjills.

435. What is the nickname of Coastal Carolina?

Chanticleers.

436. What are the three nicknames of Georgia Tech?

Ramblin' Wreck, Engineers and Yellowjackets.

437. What are the three nicknames of Auburn?

Tigers, War Eagles and Plainsmen.

438. What are the two nicknames of Yale?

Bulldogs and Elis.

439. Besides its official nickname, what school's teams are known as "The Black Knights of the Hudson?"

U.S. Military Academy.

440. Before the school's nickname was changed to Cardinal, what were Stanford's teams known as?

Indians.

441. From 1943-45 the NCAA and NIT champions played a benefit game for the Red Cross. How many times did the NCAA champs win the game?

All three times. (Wyoming beat St. John's, Utah beat St. John's, and Oklahoma A&M beat DePaul.)

442. What school led the nation in scoring three years in a row, culminating with a record 122.4-point average in 1989-90?

Loyola Marymount (Los Angeles)

443. From 1921 to 1959, the Pac-8 (and other names) had nine schools. Which of those schools is not a member of the Pac-10?

Idaho.

444. In 1978 what two schools left the Western Athletic Conference and what league did they join?

Arizona and Arizona State joined the Pac-8, making it the Pac-10.

445. What school dropped out of the Big Ten in 1946?

Chicago.

446. What school joined the Big Ten in 1949 to make it whole again?

Michigan State.

447. True or False? Northwestern never has won the Big Ten title?

False. It won in 1931 and 1933.

448. What are the only three independent schools in Division I?

Oral Roberts, Southern Utah and Wofford.

449. Since 1976, only two schools have led the nation in total home attendance in a season. Name those schools.

Kentucky and Syracuse.

450. What's the biggest crowd to attend a college game?

68,112 at the Louisiana Superdome in 1990 (LSU vs. Notre Dame).

Match these schools to their former conference:

451. Arizona State   a. Southwestern
452. South Carolina   b. Western Athletic
453. Arkansas   c. Big West
454. Penn State   d. Big East
455. UNLV   e. Atlantic Coast

451. b, 452. e, 453. a, 454. d, 455. c.

456. Name the cities that have teams in the Wisconsin State University Conference.

Eau Claire, LaCrosse, Platteville, Oshkosh, River Falls, Stevens Point, Stout, Superior and Whitewater.

457. Miami (Florida) is in what city?

Coral Gables, Fla.

458. Miami (Ohio) is in what city?

Oxford, Ohio.

459. The last time schools were allowed to play in the NCAA tournament and season-ending NIT was 1952. Name one of the three teams that played in both tourneys that year.

St. John's, Dayton and Duquesne.

460. What are the only two Pac-10 teams to win the NIT?

Stanford in 1991 and UCLA in 1985.

461. When was the last time two unbeaten schools made the Final Four?

1976, Rutgers and Indiana.

462. What was the last school to go undefeated for an entire season?

1975-76 Indiana.

463. What is the record for most victories in one season?

37 by Duke (1986) and UNLV (1987).

464. What was the last school to win the NCAA Final in its home state?

UCLA at San Diego in 1975.

465. When was the first time two schools from the same state played in the NCAA Final?

1961, Ohio State vs. Cincinnati.

466. Since 1976, three different schools in Indiana have led the nation in winning percentage in a season. Name the three schools.

Indiana (1976), Indiana State (1979) and Ball State (1989).

467. What four schools annually played in the Big Four Tournament?

North Carolina, North Carolina State, Duke and Wake Forest.

468. What school won the first National JuCo Tournament in 1946?

Pasadena College.

469. What NAIA school averaged more than 100 points a game for four straight seasons from 1954-58?

West Virginia Tech.

470. What two schools are the only ones to win three consecutive NAIA tournaments?

Tennessee State, 1957-59, and Kentucky State, 1970-72.

471. What NAIA school upset No. 1 ranked Virginia in 1982?

Chaminade (Hawaii).

472. What made the 1955 Minnesota-Purdue game so unique?

It was the longest game in Big Ten history (six overtimes), yet each team used only six players.

473. In John Wooden's last 14 seasons at UCLA, he won 13 conference titles. What school interrupted that run in 1965-66?

Oregon State.

474. When was the first telecast of the NCAA Final?

1946 from Madison Square Garden to the New York market.

475. The 1962 NCAA Final was a repeat of the 1961 Final. What were the two teams and who won both times?

Cincinnati beat Ohio State.

476. What shot was banned from college basketball from 1967-76?

The dunk.

477. What is the last wire service top 10 team to play in the NIT?

North Carolina in 1974.

478. What two teams have won at least one NCAA title in four different decades?

Kentucky in the 1990s, 1970s, 1950s and 1940s; and Indiana in the 1980s, 1970s, 1950s and 1940s.

479. What school is the only one to score more than 100 points in the NCAA title game?

UNLV in 1990.

480. What team played just five players for the entire game in winning the championship in 1963?

Loyola (Illinois).

481. When was the first time two teams from the same conference played each other in the NCAA tournament?

1944, Iowa State and Missouri.

482. What college is credited with being the first to play a full schedule of games in 1894?

Chicago.

Match these schools and their nicknames:

483. West Florida
484. West Liberty State
485. West Virginia
486. Westfield State
487. West Chester
488. Western Connecticut State
489. Western Michigan
490. Western Carolina
491. Western Maryland
492. Western Illinois

a. Hilltoppers
b. Mountaineers
c. Green Terror
d. Leathernecks
e. Catamounts
f. Golden Rams
g. Argonauts
h. Owls
i. Colonials
j. Broncos

483. g, 484. a, 485. b, 486. h, 487. f, 488. i, 489. j, 490. e, 491. c, 492. d.

COLLEGE PLAYERS

493. Who broke Bob Pettit's scoring records at LSU?

Pete Maravich.

494. Pete Maravich attended three high schools. Name one.

Daniels (Clemson, S.C.), Needham Broughton (Raleigh, N.C.) and Edwards Military Institute (Salemburg, N.C.).

495. Only once in his college career was Pete Maravich outscored by a teammate. Who accomplished this task and how many points did he score?

Danny Hester had 30 points, Maravich 20.

496. Pete Maravich averaged more than 40 points a game in his career, but what was his lowest average for a single season?

He averaged "only" 43.8 points as a sophomore in 1967-68.

497. Who ranks second behind Pete Maravich on the college career scoring list?

Freeman Williams of Portland State.

498. Who broke Julius Erving's scoring records at the University of Massachusetts?

Marcus Camby.

499. What Duke All-American broke Wilt Chamberlain's Philadelphia area high school scoring records?

Gene Banks.

500. Who scored the winning field goal when California beat Jerry West and West Virginia in the 1959 championship game?

Darrall Imhoff.

501. Name the brother combination at St. Bonaventure in 1959-60 that set a record by averaging 52 points per game.

Tom Stith (31.5 ppg) and Sam Stith (20.5 ppg).

502. Who was the last player to lead Division I in scoring in back-to-back seasons?

Harry Kelly of Texas Southern in 1981-82 and 1982-83.

503. Rick Barry led the NCAA in scoring. Where did he go to school?

University of Miami (Florida).

504. What other amazing feat did Rick Barry accomplish at college?

He married the coach's daughter.

Bill Walton

505. Name Rick Barry's four sons who all played at Division I schools.

Brent, Drew, Jon and Scooter.

506. What school did Jerry Sloan attend before transferring to Evans-ville?

Illinois.

507. Who are the only three players to be named College Player of the Year three years in a row?

Oscar Robertson, Bill Walton and Ralph Sampson.

Mark Aguirre

508. How many baseball games did Larry Bird play at Indiana State?

One; he played first base.

509. How many basketball games did Deion Sanders play at Florida State?

None.

510. Mark Aguirre was the College Player of the Year at what school?

DePaul.

511. Who is the only player at UNLV to win the Player of the Year award?

Larry Johnson.

Larry Johnson

512. Who received the 1971 NCAA tournament's Outstanding Player award, then subsequently had it taken away after being declared ineligible for having an agent?

Howard Porter, Villanova.

513. Who is the only player to be named MVP of the Final Four and NIT?

Tom Gola of LaSalle.

514. Who is the only player to be selected Most Outstanding Player in the Final Four three straight years?

Lew Alcindor.

Christian Laettner

515. What two opposing players combined for the most points in a game?

LSU's Pete Maravich (64) and Kentucky's Dan Issel (51).

516. Who is the only player to start in four straight Final Fours?

Christian Laettner of Duke.

517. What was the quickest anyone has fouled out of a game?

1:38 by Mike Pflugner of Butler.

518. The 1953-54 Cincinnati team featured Jack Twyman and what other two future sports stars?

Sandy Koufax and Tony Trabert.

519. What former DePaul star is the brother of Whitney Houston?

Gary Garland.

520. What Syracuse player was the first in NCAA history to record career totals of 2,000 points, 1,500 rebounds and 300 blocked shots?

Derrick Coleman.

521. What St. John's player was featured on the cover of *Sports Illustrated* while still in high school?

Felipe Lopez.

522. Who was the first player to play for two different schools in an NCAA title game?

Bob Bender with Indiana (1976) and Duke (1978).

523. Who is the only Atlantic Coast Conference player to lead the nation in scoring?

South Carolina's Grady Wallace in 1956-57.

524. What native of the island nation of the Grenadines holds the Division I record for most blocked shots in a career?

Adonal Foyle of Colgate.

525. What LaSalle star still holds after 40 years the Division I record for career rebounds?

Tom Gola.

526. What Indiana All-American broke his arm, possibly depriving the Hoosiers from an undefeated season and national championship in 1975?

Scott May.

527. How many points did Furman's Frank Selvy score to set the Division I single game record?

100.

528. Who holds the Division I single game scoring record against another D-I school?

Kevin Bradshaw of U.S. International, 72 points.

529. Kevin Bradshaw transferred to USIU from what small Florida school?

Bethune-Cookman.

530. Who is the only Division I player to average more than 25 points a game in each of his four varsity seasons?

Alphonso Ford of Mississippi Valley State, 1989-93.

531. What Penn State dead-eye broke UCLA's Rod Foster's single season free throw accuracy record in 1984-85?

Craig Collins (94 of 98).

532. What three players led Division I players in scoring and rebounding in the same season?

Xavier McDaniel

Xavier McDaniel (Wichita State), Hank Gathers (Loyola Marymount) and Kurt Thomas (Texas Christian).

533. Who was the Wooden Award winner that led Arizona to its first Final Four appearance?

Sean Elliott.

534. Who was the first African-American to receive a basketball scholarship at North Carolina?

Charlie Scott.

535. Who is the only player to have career averages of more than 22 points and 22 rebounds a game?

Artis Gilmore.

536. Who was the last player to average 20 points and 20 rebounds in a season?

Kermit Washington of American.

537. Who was the first collegian to surpass the 1,000-point mark in a career?

John Roosma of Army in 1926.

538. Who averaged a record 52.7 points in three NCAA tourney games?

Austin Carr of Notre Dame.

539. Who holds the record for most points scored in an NCAA tourney?

Glen Rice of Michigan, 184 points in six games.

540. Who holds the record for most points in a career in the NCAA tourney?

Christian Laettner of Duke, 407 points in 23 games.

541. Who holds the record for the highest career scoring average (minimum of 10 games) in the NCAA tourney?

Oscar Robertson of Cincinnati, 32.4 points per game.

Bobby Hurley

542. Who holds the record for most points scored in an NCAA tournament game?

Austin Carr, 61 points.

543. What Duke Blue Devil holds the record for most career assists in the NCAA tourney?

Bobby Hurley.

544. What Houston Cougar holds the record for most career rebounds in the NCAA tourney?

Elvin Hayes.

545. Who was the last player to win the NCAA tournament's Most Outstanding Player award that wasn't on the championship team?

Akeem Olajuwon of Houston in 1983.

546. Who was the first player to earn consensus All-American honors three years in a row?

John Wooden of Purdue.

547. Where was Danny Ferry's father, Bob, a star player?

St. Louis.

548. Where was Kiki Vandeweghe's father, Ernie, a star player?

Colgate.

549. Who was the back-up center at UCLA who went on to lead the ABA in rebounding in 1974-75?

Swen Nater.

Kiki Vandeweghe

550. Which UCLA star did John Wooden praise as "the greatest all-around player I've coached."

Gail Goodrich.

551. Who joined Sidney Wicks at forward for three straight seasons at UCLA?

Curtis Rowe.

552. He did not write *American Pie*, but who did score 2,608 points in his UCLA career?

Don MacLean.

Akeem Olajuwon

553. Who was the starter at UCLA from 1965-68 who never played in the NBA, but did become a popular television star?

Mike Warren of Hill Street Blues

554. Where did 1968 Olympic shot put champion Randy Matson play one season of varsity basketball?

Texas A&M.

555. Where was baseball Hall of Famer Bob Gibson a standout basketball player?

Creighton.

556. Who was the Duke basketball All-American who wound up leading the National League in hitting?

Dick Groat.

557. Who pitched a no-hitter for the Cleveland Indians and led Missouri in scoring in 1957-58?

Sonny Siebert.

558. Who is the only person to win an NCAA basketball championship and Major League Baseball World Series?

Pete Stoddard at North Carolina State and for the Baltimore Orioles.

559. At what Big Ten school was baseball slugger Frank Howard also a basketball standout?

Ohio State.

560. What future San Francisco 49er wide receiver was a teammate of Elgin Baylor at Idaho?

R.C. Owens.

561. What future Buffalo Bill was named the Most Outstanding Player of the 1982 Division III tournament?

Pete Metzelaars of Wabash.

562. What Notre Dame quarterback scored the final 11 points as Notre Dame beat a Kentucky team that went on to win the NIT in 1946?

George Ratterman.

563. What college roommate of Tommy Lee Jones averaged 2.8 points a game for Harvard's freshman team in 1965-66?

Al Gore.

564. What former presidential candidate played on the Kansas freshman team before an injury in World War II cut short his athletic career?

Bob Dole.

565. What future Secretary of the Interior led his Arizona team to the NIT in 1946?

Stewart Udall.

566. Name Michigan's "Fab Five."

Juwan Howard, Jalen Rose, Chris Webber, Jimmy King and Ray Jackson.

567. The 1970 national runner-up, Jacksonville, featured a front line that averaged 7-feet. Name the three players and their heights.

Artis Gilmore, 7-foot-2; Pembrook Burrows, 7-0; and Rod McIntyre, 6-10.

568. The 1989-90 LSU team featured two 7-foot centers that weighed in over 600 pounds. Name them.

Stanley Roberts and Shaquille O'Neal.

569. Often overlooked, who was the fifth starter on North Carolina State's 1974 championship team that boasted David Thompson, Tom Burleson, Monte Towe and Tim Stoddard?

Moe Rivers, a junior guard who averaged 12 points a game.

Shaquille O'Neal

570. Name three of the six players who averaged double-figures for UNLV's 1977 Final Four team.

Lewis Brown, Glen Gondrezick, Eddie Owens, Robert Smith, Sam Smith and Reggie Theus.

571. What Brigham Young center left school to spend two years on a Mormon mission in Australia?

Shawn Bradley.

572. What player and the Texas Longhorn share the same nickname? Oh, and by the way, he scored 113 points in a game.

Clarence "Bevo" Francis of Rio Grande College.

573. "Bevo" Francis scored his 113 points against what team?

Hillsdale College.

574. How many points did "Bevo" Francis score in the 1952-53 season?

1954.

575. What famous small school "football factory" did Willis Reed attend?

Grambling.

576. Who are the two Furman players among the top 10 on the Division I all-time career scoring average list?

Frank Selvy and Darrell Floyd.

577. Starting in 1954-55, West Virginia had three successive All-America guards that played three successive seasons. Name them.

"Hot" Rod Hundley, 1954-57; Jerry West, 1957-60; and Rod Thorn, 1960-63.

578. What freshman holds the Division I record for highest scoring average?

Chris Jackson of LSU (30.2 points per game).

579. Who was the first player to score 1,000 career points?

Christian Steinmetz of Wisconsin.

580. Who was the first player to score 2,000 career points?

Jim Lacy of Loyola (Md.).

581. Who was the first player to score 3,000 career points?

Pete Maravich of LSU.

582. Who was the star of Grand Canyon College's 1978 NAIA championship team?

Bayard Forest.

583. Name the highest scoring trio on one team in one season. Hint: It was in 1989-90.

Loyola Marymount's Bo Kimble (33.5 points per game), Hank Gathers (29.0 ppg) and Jeff Fryar (22.7 ppg).

584. Hank Gathers and Bo Kimble both started at what school before transferring to Loyola Marymount?

U. of Southern California.

585. What Loyola Marymount player collapsed and died in a 1990 West Coast Conference game?

Hank Gathers.

586. Who was the first player in NCAA history to rank in the top five nationally in scoring, assists and steals in the same season?

Terrell Lowery of Loyola Marymount.

587. Only two players in Atlantic Coast Conference history have 2,000 points and 600 assists. One is from North Carolina and the other is from Georgia Tech. Name them.

Phil Ford and Travis Best.

588. Who was the high-flying bird that led Division I players in scoring in 1972-73?

William "Bird" Averitt of Pepperdine.

589. Who was the first consensus All-American at Michigan?

Cazzie Russell.

590. Who is the only consensus All-American at Illinois State?

Doug Collins.

Jack Sikma

591. Who is the only consensus All-American at Vanderbilt?

Clyde Lee.

592. What three-time academic All-American played at Illinois Wesleyan?

Jack Sikma.

593. Who is the only three-time academic All-American at Santa Clara?

Dennis Awtrey.

594. David Robinson was the second consensus All-American at Navy. Who was the first?

Elliott Loughlin in 1933.

595. What is God Shammgod's original name?

God Shammgod.

596. What did Rhode Island's two-time All-American Stan Modzelewski change his name to?

Stan Stutz.

597. What southwestern college player of the late 1970s shared a last name with a famous Greek philosopher?

Tony Zeno.

598. What North Carolina player shares a name with Gomer Pyle's sergeant?

Vince Carter.

599. True or False? Michael Jordan never made first-team all-Atlantic Coast Conference.

False.

600. Michael Jordan scored 16 points in North Carolina's win over Georgetown in the 1982 NCAA Final, but what Tar Heel scored 28 points?

James Worthy.

601. Who was the first player to lead the Final Four in scoring while playing on the championship team?

Jim Pollard of Stanford in 1942.

602. Who is the only Division I regular season scoring champion to play on the championship team?

Clyde Lovellette of Kansas.

603. Who is the last Big Ten player to lead the nation in scoring?

Glenn Robinson of Purdue.

604. What Stanford player was named MVP of the 1942 Final Four?

Howie Dallmar.

605. What Stanford player is credited with pioneering the jump shot in the 1930s?

Angelo "Hank" Luisetti.

606. Who was the first freshman to be named Most Outstanding Player in the Final Four?

Arnie Ferrin of Utah, 1944.

607. What center blocked 207 shots in 1985-86 which bested the team totals of every college except his own and the national championship team, Louisville?

David Robinson.

David Robinson

608. What Prairie View player led Division I three-point field goal shooters in accuracy in 1986-87, the first year the bonus shot was used?

Reginald Jones.

609. Who is the only player besides Lew Alcindor to score more than 2,000 points in only three Pac-10 seasons. Hint: The Southern Cal star was dubbed "Baby Jordan."

Harold Miner.

610. In 1957-58, four of the top eight Division I scorers went on to become NBA All-Stars. Name them.

Oscar Robertson (No. 1), Elgin Baylor (No. 3), Wilt Chamberlain (No. 5) and Bailey Howell (No. 8).

611. In 1952 Grantland Rice conducted a poll to name the top five college all-stars of the half century. Name three of the team members.

Hank Luisetti (Stanford), George Mikan (DePaul), John Wooden (Purdue), Bob Kurland (Oklahoma State) and Vic Hanson (Syracuse).

Moses Malone

612. Who were the only three college players chosen in the original 1959 induction class of the Naismith Hall of Fame?

George Mikan, Hank Luisetti and Charles Hyatt.

613. If he had not turned pro right out of high school, where was Moses Malone going to attend college?

Maryland.

614. For what school did Rick Mount sign a letter of intent before changing his mind and enrolling at Purdue?

Miami (Florida)

615. What Southeastern Conference school originally signed Spencer Haywood, but could not get him enrolled because of the league's entrance requirements?

Tennessee.

616. What school did Bill Bradley publicly announce he would attend before opting for Princeton?

Duke.

617. Bill Russell chose San Francisco over how many other colleges that recruited him?

Zero.

618. Who was headed to his hometown school, Louisville, but instead followed his father who earned an assistant coaching job at Tennessee?

Allan Houston.

619. Who is Arkansas's career rebounding leader?

Sidney Moncrief.

620. Who is Stanford's career scoring leader?

Todd Lichti.

621. Who is Virginia's career scoring leader?

Bryant Stith.

622. What Texas player will forever be the Southwest Conference career scoring leader now that the league is defunct?

Terrence Rencher.

623. What McNeese State star led the Southland Conference in scoring three years in a row?

Joe Dumars.

624. Who are the only three 7-footers to lead the nation in rebounding?

Artis Gilmore, Akeem Olajuwon and Shaquille O'Neal.

625. Robert Parish was the "Gent" from where?

Centenary.

Robert Parrish

626. Besides punter Ray Guy, who is the only other athlete to have his uniform number retired at Southern Mississippi?

Clarence Weatherspoon.

627. What gravelly voiced announcer was a three-time All-Southeastern Conference pick at LSU and later returned to his alma mater as the athletic director?

Joe Dean.

Match these players with the colleges they attended:

628. Kresimir Cosic   a. Purdue
629. Dan Majerle   b. Marquette
630. Dave Cowens   c. Brigham Young
631. Freeman Williams   d. UCLA
632. Tom Gola   e. LaSalle
633. Rick Mount   f. Central Michigan
634. Butch Lee   g. Ohio State
635. Gary Bradds   h. Oregon State
636. Steve Johnson   i. Portland State
637. Walt Hazzard   j. Florida State

628. c, 629. f, 630. j, 631. i, 632. e, 633. a, 634. b, 635. g, 636. h, 637. d.

Match these players with the colleges they first attended:

638. Kyle Macy   a. Duke
639. Elgin Baylor   b. Kentucky
640. Greg Starrick   c. Idaho
641. Gus Johnson   d. Northwestern
642. Lindsey Hunter   e. Purdue
643. George Gervin   f. Long Beach State
644. Avery Johnson   g. North Carolina
645. Rex Walters   h. Cameron
646. Clifford Rozier   i. Alcorn State
647. Billy McCaffrey   j. Akron

638. e, 639. c, 640. b, 641. j, 642. i, 643. f, 644. h, 645. d, 646. g, 647. a.

Match these players with the junior colleges they attended:

648. Bob McAdoo   a. Odessa, Texas
649. Larry Johnson   b. Midland, Texas
650. Bill Laimbeer   c. Gardner-Webb, North Carolina
651. Artis Gilmore   d. Cooke County, Texas
652. Mookie Blaylock   e. Vincennes, Indiana
653. Charlie Ward   f. Tallahassee, Florida
654. Spencer Haywood   g. Trinity Valley, Texas
655. Ricky Pierce   h. Trinidad State, Colorado
656. Dennis Rodman   i. Owens Tech, Ohio
657. Nick Van Exel   j. Walla Walla, Washington
658. Latrell Sprewell   k. Three Rivers, Missouri

648. e, 649. a, 650. i, 651. c, 652. b, 653. f, 654. h, 655. j,
656. d, 657. g.

Match these top career rebounders with their schools:

659. Tom Gola   a. Connecticut
660. Joe Holup   b. Morehead State
661. Charlie Slack   c. LaSalle
662. Ed Conlin   d. William & Mary
663. Dickie Hemric   e. George Washington
664. Paul Silas   f. Creighton
665. Art Quimby   g. Alabama
666. Jerry Harper   h. Marshall
667. Jeff Cohen   i. Wake Forest
668. Steve Hamilton   j. Fordham

659. c, 660. e, 661. h, 662. j, 663. i, 664. f, 665. a, 666. g,
667. d, 668. b.

COLLEGE COACHES

669. Who spent 39 years as a college head coach before he was honored as Coach of the Year in 1983-84?

Marv Harshman.

670. In 1986, who left Western Kentucky, his alma mater, to become head coach of a Big Ten school he would lead to the Final Four 11 years later?

Clem Haskins.

671. Who are the three former star players who now are head coaches at Iona, Houston and Texas Tech?

Jeff Ruland, Clyde Drexler and Jeff Lebo.

672. Which of the three coaches above is not an alumnus of the school where he coaches today, and where did he go to college?

Jeff Lebo, North Carolina.

673. Name the two colleges where Larry Brown was head coach.

UCLA and Kansas.

674. Name the three colleges where Rick Pitino was head coach.

Boston U., Providence, Kentucky.

Rick Pitino

675. Name one of the four colleges where Bill Fitch was head coach.

Coe, North Dakota, Bowling Green, Minnesota.

676. What school did Bill Sharman coach in the early 1960s?

Cal State-Los Angeles.

677. What Boston Celtics legend was the head coach at Boston College?

Bob Cousy.

678. Ed "Moose" Krause was an All-American player, the head coach for five years, then the long-time athletic director of what school?

Notre Dame.

679. Fill in the blank. Lefty Driesell promised to make the University of Maryland "the _____ of the East."

UCLA.

680. What two schools did Gene Bartow coach before taking Memphis State to the NCAA final in 1973?

Valparaiso and Central Missouri State.

681. What is former Alabama coach Wimp Sanders' real first name?

Winfrey.

682. Who is the only person to play on an NBA championship team and coach an NCAA title winner?

John Thompson.

683. Who are the only three coaches to guide teams into the Final Four and NBA Finals?

Jack Ramsay, Fred Schaus and Bill van Breda Kolff.

684. Whose career victories record did Dean Smith break?

Adolph Rupp.

685. Whose career victories record did Adolph Rupp break?

Ed Diddle.

686. Whose career victories record did Ed Diddle break?

Phog Allen.

687. Where did Adolph Rupp coach immediately prior to the University of Kentucky?

Freeport (Illinois) High School.

688. Dean Smith devised the Four Corners spread offense while he was assistant coach at what school?

Air Force. Because of the academy's height restrictions, the offense was created to neutralize the height advantage of other schools.

689. In Dean Smith's second season as head coach at North Carolina, what future NBA coach was his captain?

Larry Brown.

690. In Dean Smith's fourth season at North Carolina, what future NBA coach was his captain?

Billy Cunningham.

691. In the 1970s, the Atlantic Coast Conference had two coaches with the same name. Who were they and where did they coach?

Bill Foster, Duke and Bill Foster, Clemson.

692. What Atlantic Coast Conference school did Bobby Cremins attend?

South Carolina, prior to leaving the ACC.

693. Who was the first coach to take two different schools to the NCAA championship game?

Frank McGuire with St. John's (1952) and North Carolina (1957).

694. Where was Red Auerbach an assistant coach in 1949-50?

Duke.

695. Who was the coach, known as "The Fox," who first led Arizona to prominence?

Fred Snowden.

696. Who was the coach in just his second season that led a Big Ten school to the 1960 NCAA title?

Fred Taylor.

697. Who is the only coach to win an NCAA championship as a player and head coach?

Bob Knight.

698. Where was John Wooden's first college head coaching job?

Indiana State.

699. How many seasons was John Wooden the head coach at UCLA before he won his first NCAA title?

Sixteen.

700. Who is the only Division I coach to go undefeated in his first season as a head coach?

Norman Shepard, at North Carolina in 1923-24.

701. Who is the only coach to take four different schools to the NCAA tournament?

Eddie Sutton (Creighton, Arkansas, Kentucky and Oklahoma State).

702. What is the record for most seasons as head coach at one school?

42, by Ed Diddle at Western Kentucky and Ray Meyer at DePaul.

703. Former Duke play maker Tommy Amaker is the head coach at what school?

Seton Hall.

704. Who is the former coach at Arizona State that was the starting center at UCLA between Lew Alcindor and Bill Walton?

Steve Patterson.

705. Who replaced Bill Frieder as head coach prior to the start of the 1989 NCAA tournament, then led Michigan to the championship?

Steve Fisher.

706. Who took over for Missouri in the 1989 tournament after Norm Stewart became ill?

Rich Daly.

707. When he began his coaching career, John Thompson actually held down two coaching jobs at once. Where?

The District of Columbia; at Federal City College and St. Anthony's High School.

708. Since John Wooden, who is the only coach to win back-to-back national titles?

Mike Krzyzewski of Duke.

709. Who was Cincinnati's coach when it won back-to-back titles in 1961-62?

Edwin Jucker.

710. What coach was at St. John's for 11 years, the New York Knicks for nine years, then back at St. John's for another 9 seasons?

Joe Lapchick.

711. Where did Lou Henson coach from 1962-66 before going to New Mexico State?

Hardin-Simmons.

712. What was Lou Henson's salary when he returned to New Mexico State in 1997?

$1 per month.

713. Who was the interim head coach at California replacing Lou Campanelli in 1993, then getting replaced himself in 1996 by Ben Brown?

Todd Bozeman.

714. At UNLV in 1994-95—the first losing season in 35 years—the school used four different head coaches. Name two of them.

Rollie Massimino (who quit just before the start of fall practice), Tim Grgurich (who quit in January after being admitted to a hospital for exhaustion), Howie Landa (who claimed "burn out" after just seven games) and Cle Edwards (who finished the season).

715. Where was Norm Sloan the head coach from 1957-60?

The Citadel.

716. Where was Billy Packer an assistant coach under Jack McKinney?

Wake Forest.

717. Where were Eddie Sutton, Don Haskins, Moe Iba and Jack Hartman all assistant coaches?

Oklahoma State.

718. What school did Jack Hartman coach to the 1967 NIT championship?

Southern Illinois.

719. Who was the star of that Southern Illinois team?

Walt Frazier.

720. Guy Lewis was the head coach for 30 years at what school?

Houston.

721. Who was the first African-American head coach in the Atlantic Coast Conference?

Bob Wade at Maryland in 1986-87.

722. Three of the seven winningest coaches of all-time graduated from the same school. What is that cradle of coaches?

Kansas (Smith, Rupp and Allen).

723. What famous coaches went by the names Taps, Nibs and Piggy?

Taps Gallagher (Niagara), Nibs Price (California) and Piggy Lambert (Purdue).

724. Who is the only person to play on an NIT championship team and coach an NIT championship team?

Jeff Jones, both times at Virginia (1980 and '92).

725. Since 1981, who is the only coach to win two UPI Coach of the Year awards?

Norm Stewart of Missouri.

726. In between coaching at San Francisco and California, where was Pete Newell the head coach for four years?

Michigan State.

727. Who are the only two coaches that are the winningest coaches at two different Division I schools?

Ralph Miller at Wichita State and Oregon State, and Johnny Orr at Michigan and Iowa State.

728. Who won the first national Coach of the Year award in 1955?

Phil Woolpert of San Francisco.

729. Who won the 1977 NCAA championship in his final game as a head coach?

Al McGuire at Marquette.

730. Where was Al McGuire coaching for seven years before going to Marquette?

Belmont Abbey.

731. Where did Lute Olson make his college head coaching debut in 1973?

Long Beach State.

732. Where did Pete Carril coach before going to Princeton in 1967?

Lehigh.

733. What three schools did Jim Valvano coach before going to North Carolina State?

Johns Hopkins, Bucknell and Iona.

734. Where was Dick Vitale's last college coaching job?

University of Detroit.

735. Who is the only coach besides Dean Smith and Adolph Rupp to win 800 games at a four-year school?

Clarence "Big House" Gaines, at Winston-Salem State.

736. Who was Larry Bird's head coach in his final season at Indiana State?

Bill Hodges.

737. Who was Magic Johnson's head coach in his final season at Michigan State?

Jud Heathcote.

738. Who was Michael Jordan's head coach in his final season at North Carolina?

Dean Smith.

Match these legendary coaches with the school they coached:

739. Tony Hinkle
740. Aubrey Bonham
741. Robert Vaughan
742. Herb Magee
743. Ken Anderson
744. Dean Nicholson
745. Dom Rosselli
746. Joe Hutton
747. Fred Hobdy
748. Glenn Wilkes

a. Wisconsin-Eau Claire
b. Philadelphia Textile
c. Elizabeth City State
d. Whittier
e. Hamline
f. Central Washington
g. Grambling
h. Butler
i. Youngstown State
j. Stetson

739. h, 740. d, 741. c, 742. b, 743. a, 744. f, 745. i, 746. e, 747. g, 748. j.

COLLEGE ARENAS

Q.

749. Pauley Pavilion is one of the most recognized names in college sports. Who was Pauley?

Edwin W. Pauley was the main benefactor during the construction of the UCLA building.

750. Because their gym had been ruled unsafe for more than 1,000 people, UCLA spent 10 seasons (1956-66) playing home games in a variety of places. Name any of them.

Venice High School, Pan-Pacific Auditorium, Long Beach Arena, Long Beach City College, Los Angeles Sports Arena and Santa Monica City College.

751. Where was the first NCAA Final Four in 1939?

Patten Gymnasium at Evanston, Illinois.

752. True or False. The NCAA Final Four never has been held in New York City.

False. It was there from 1943-48 and again in 1950.

753. For nearly 40 years the College Division (Division II) championship was held at only two cities. Name them.

Evansville, Indiana and Springfield, Massachusetts.

754. Gill Coliseum houses what animals?

The Beavers of Oregon State.

755. What was the first foreign team to play in Madison Square Garden?

University of Havana, Cuba, lost to Long Island University in the 1943-44 season.

756. For more than 40 years since it was built in 1927, what was the largest on-campus arena?

Minnesota's Williams Arena (20,176 seats).

757. What school uses the largest arena on a regular basis?

Syracuse, Carrier Dome (33,000 seats).

758. What two Big 10 schools have the same name of their arenas? Hint: They also both play football in "Memorial Stadium."

Illinois and Indiana.

Match these arenas with their colleges:

759. Diddle Arena   a. Temple
760. Thompson-Boling Arena   b. Harvard
761. Crisler Arena   c. California
762. Harmon Gym   d. Maryland
763. Cole Field House   e. Western Kentucky
764. The Forum at the Apollo   f. Michigan
765. Lloyd Noble Center   g. Tennessee
766. Bud Walton Arena   h. Evansville
767. Lavietes Pavilion   i. Arkansas
768. Roberts Stadium   j. Oklahoma

759. e, 760. g, 761. f, 762. c, 763. d, 764. a, 765. j, 766. i, 767. b, 768. h.

769. Who led the 1992 U.S. Dream Team in scoring?

Charles Barkley (18.0 points per game).

770. Who were the four North Carolina Tar Heels on the 1976 U.S. team coached by Dean Smith?

Walter Davis, Phil Ford, Mitch Kupchak and Tom LaGarde.

771. When was the last time an AAU player was named to the U.S. team?

1972, Kenny Davis of Marathon Oil.

772. What two teams filled the 10-player roster of the 1948 U.S. team?

Phillips Oilers and Kentucky each had five players on the team.

Adrian Dantley

773. Who holds the U.S. record for the highest scoring average?

Adrian Dantley (19.3 points per game in 1976).

774. Who was the first African-American on the U.S. team?

Don Barksdale.

775. Dan Majerle played on which bronze-medal winning U.S. team?

1988.

776. Toni Kukoc was a member of what Olympic teams?

1988 Yugoslavia, 1992 and 1996 Croatia.

Dan Majerle

777. Arvydas Sabonis was a member of what Olympic teams?

1988 U.S.S.R., 1992 and 1996 Lithuania.

778. What 7-foot Soviet woman won two gold medals and is a member of the Naismith Basketball Hall of Fame?

Juliana Semenova.

779. What male Soviet Olympic hero was the first international player elected to the Hall of Fame?

Toni Kukoc

Sergei Belov.

780. What current NBA player was a member of the 1984 West German team?

Detlef Schrempf.

Detlef Schrempf

Patrick Ewing

781. Who was born in Jamaica, but started at center for the 1984 and 1992 U.S. teams?

Patrick Ewing.

782. In 1964 UCLA starting forward Keith Erickson represented the U.S. in what sport?

Volleyball.

783. Lew Alcindor's high school coach, Jack Donohue, was the head coach of what Olympic team in 1984?

Canada.

784. Who were the starting players on the 1960 U.S. team?

Oscar Robertson, Jerry West, Terry Dischinger, Jerry Lucas and Walt Bellamy.

785. What country did the U.S. beat in the first Olympic final at Berlin in 1936?

Canada, 19-8, outdoors in the rain.

786. So, when was the first basketball game played in the Olympics?

1904, as an exhibition sport at St. Louis.

787. When was the first time the U.S. played the U.S.S.R. in the Olympics?

1952 at Helsinki.

788. Before the U.S. lost at Munich, what was the closest score the Americans had?

U.S. 2, Spain 0, a forfeit at Berlin in 1936.

789. Why did Spain forfeit?

Because of the Spanish Civil War, the team never showed up.

790. What was the closest game that actually was played?

U.S. 59, Argentina 57, at London in 1948.

791. Who is Bradley's all-time leading scoring that was a member of the 1988 U.S. team?

Hersey Hawkins.

792. Who was the last junior college player to make the U.S. team?

Tom Henderson.

WHO AM I?

793. I drove a garbage truck.
I transferred from Indiana to Northwood Institute.
I'm known as "The Hick from French Lick."

Larry Bird.

794. My "old" first name was Ferdinand.
I attended Power Memorial High School.
I scored more points than any NBA player in history.

Kareem Abdul-Jabbar.

795. I attended Power Memorial High School.
I have played professionally in Portugal, Argentina, Ireland, the USBL, CBA and WBL.
I was a member of two NBA championship teams at Houston.

Mario Elie.

796. My uncle was a six-time all-star game participant.
I followed him to his alma mater.
I was a first-round draft pick of the New York Knicks in 1992.

Hubert Davis.

797. I was a first-round draft choice of the Dallas Mavericks in 1980.
My father, Ernie, played in the NBA.
My mother, Colleen, was Miss America.

Kiki Vandeweghe.

798. I am a member of the NBA's 50th anniversary all-star team.
I teamed with my former college teammate to win an NBA title.
I retired from playing and became the head coach at my alma mater.

Clyde Drexler.

799. I was the first star 7-foot player.
I was named outstanding player of the Final Four twice.
I played AAU ball, but never in the NBA.

Bob Kurland.

800. I'm the all-time high school scoring leader in Alaska.
I spent my college summers playing for the San Diego Padres organization.
I was named for a Roman emperor.

Trajan Langdon.

801. I played in both the Rose Bowl and Final Four for Illinois.
I finished tied for second in the high jump at the 1948 Olympics.
I was a two-time NBA all-star.

Dike Eddleman.

802. I was a starter in basketball for Illinois.
I won the American League MVP in 1948.
I am a long-time announcer for the Chicago Cubs.

Lou Boudreau.

803. I played only one year of varsity basketball at Washington State.
I won 91 games in the major leagues.
I played six years in the NBA.

Gene Conley.

804. I participated in football, basketball, baseball and track at UCLA.
I am in the National Baseball Hall of Fame.
My uniform number now is retired by all major league teams.

Jackie Robinson.

805. I was the second-leading scorer for a Final Four team.
I won the Heisman Trophy.
I played in the Canadian Football League.

Terry Baker.

806. I was an All-American at Princeton.
I played on two NBA championship teams with the New York Knicks.
I share the same name as a 1970s all-pro safety of the Philadelphia Eagles.

Bill Bradley.

807. I was an All-American at Purdue.
I succeeded Wilbur Johns as coach.
I won 10 NCAA titles as a coach.

John Wooden.

808. I was born in Detroit.
I played at Austin Catholic High School in Detroit.
I played at the University of Detroit.
I played for the Detroit Pistons.

Dave DeBusschere.

809. I went to high school in Washington, D.C., and attended Syracuse.
I led the NBA in scoring in my second season.
I own a successful steel products company.

Dave Bing.

810. I was born in Johannesburg, South Africa.
I played high school basketball in Victory, British Columbia.
I attended Santa Clara University in the U.S.

Steve Nash.

811. I played high school basketball at Middletown, Ohio.
I was a three-time first-team All-American at
Ohio State.
I sat out a year rather than sign with the
Cincinnati Royals.

Jerry Lucas.

812. I was the first player to break a backboard in an NBA game.
I hit a home run at Dodger Stadium.
I played the Rifleman.

Chuck Conners

813. I was a coach at Providence in the 1970s.
I was Big East commissioner in the 1980s.
I was president of the Boston Celtics in the 1990s.

Dave Gavitt.

Dave Gavitt

814. I served two years in the Army, immediately following college.
I was drafted by the then-Los Angeles Rams.
I have played on NCAA, NBA and Olympic championship teams.

K.C. Jones.

815. I own the Seattle Seahawks.
I own the Portland Trail Blazers.
I am the third richest man in the U.S.

Paul Allen.

816. My father played for three NBA and three ABA teams.
I was the college Player of the Year as a senior.
I was the first overall pick in the 1988 NBA draft.

Danny Manning.

817. I was the college Player of the Year at UCLA.
My brother played for the Milwaukee Bucks.
I married Don Drysdale.

Ann Meyers.

818. My brother plays in the NBA.
Another brother played Major League Baseball.
I'm a head coach in the WNBA.

Cheryl Miller.

819. I hold 14 career UCLA records.
I scored in double figures in a record 130 games.
I was a three-time All-American.

Denise Curry.

Danny Manning

Ralph Simpson or Ralph Sampson?

820. I played high school basketball with Spencer Haywood.

Ralph Simpson.

821. I played in the Final Four.

Ralph Sampson.

822. I was half of the "Twin Towers."

Ralph Sampson.

823. I left college after my sophomore season.

Ralph Simpson.

824. I was an academic All-American.

Ralph Simpson.

825. I played for my hometown NBA team.

Ralph Simpson.

826. I was traded to Golden State for Joe Barry Carroll, Sleepy Floyd and Steve Harris.

Ralph Sampson.

Q.

827. What team won the inaugural WNBA championship in 1997?

Houston Comets.

828. Who was the MVP in the WNBA's first season?

Cynthia Cooper, Houston Comets.

829. Who is president of the WNBA?

Valerie Ackerman.

830. Before the NCAA began overseeing women's college basketball, what organization was responsible for women's sports programs?

The Association of Intercollegiate Athletics for Women (AIAW).

831. What school won the first three AIAW championships from 1972-74?

Immaculata College.

832. What "major" university was the first to win an AIAW title?

UCLA in 1978.

833. What school had two members of the NCAA Team of the Decade for the 1980s?

Louisiana Tech, Janice Lawrence and Teresa Weatherspoon.

834. Who was the first woman to dunk in an NCAA game?

Georgeann Wells of West Virginia in 1984.

835. At what school did Lillian Haas coach for a record 29 years?

Drexel.

836. What school won the National Women's Invitational Tournament nine times in a row from 1969-77?

Wayland Baptist.

837. What school set the Division I record with 54 straight wins?

Louisiana Tech.

838. What school set the Division I record with 37 straight loses from 1989-92?

Southwestern Louisiana.

839. Who is the only Division I player to repeat as the national scoring champion?

Andrea Congreaves of Mercer, 1991-92 and 1992-93.

840. Who holds the Division I scoring record of 60 points in a game?

Cindy Brown, Long Beach State in 1987.

841. Who holds the Division I rebounding record of 40 in a game?

Deborah Temple, Delta State in 1983.

842. Who was the 6-foot-8 three-time All-American at Old Dominion?

Anne Donovan.

843. Who was the only high schooler on the 1976 U.S. Olympic team?

Nancy Lieberman.

844. Who is the only three-time basketball winner of the Honda-Broderick Cup given to the Collegiate Woman Athlete of the Year?

Cheryl Miller.

845. Carol "The Blaze" Blazejowski set the AIAW record of 3,199 career points while playing for what school?

Montclair State (N.J.).

846. The Division II championship is traditionally held in what northern city?

Fargo, N.D.

847. What is the only school to repeat as the Division III national champion?

Capital University (Ohio), 1994 and 1995.

848. Spell the first name of Purdue's Joseph who earned 1992 All-America honors.

MaChelle.

849. The L'eggs Classic holiday tournament is held at what southwestern school?

New Mexico State.

850. What two Southern California players scored more than 100 points in a high school game?

Cheryl Miller and Lisa Leslie.

851. What other two sports did Ann Meyers play at UCLA?

Volleyball and track & field.

852. Who was the first woman to actually play in a men's professional league?

Nancy Lieberman in the United States Basketball League in 1986.

853. Who was the first woman college coach inducted into the Naismith Basketball Hall of Fame?

Margaret Wade of Delta State.

854. What school won 188 consecutive conference games in the 1980s?

Texas in the Southwest Conference.

855. Who was the first transfer student to play for Tennessee under Coach Pat Summitt?

Michelle Marciniak who wound up the 1996 Final Four MVP.

856. Who are the two North Dakota State players who each won two Division II MVP tourney awards?

Nadine Schmidt and Kasey Morlock.

857. What team snapped Tennessee's 46-game winning streak in 1998?

Purdue.

858. Who was the Russian star who played at Connecticut in the 1990s?

Svetlana Abrosimova.

859. What school won 10 women's AAU titles from 1955-69?

Nashville Business College.

860. Who was the star of the Dallas Golden Cyclones that won the 1931 Women's AAU national championship?

Mildred "Babe" Didrikson.

Yes or No?
Did These Famous Women Play High School Basketball?

861. *Entertainment Tonight's* Julie Moran.

Yes.

862. Singer Liz Phair.

No.

863. The ex-Mrs. Donald Trump, Marla Maples.

Yes.

864. Model Cindy Crawford.

No.

865. Pro basketball star Sheryl Swoopes.

Yes.

866. ESPN's Robin Roberts.

Yes.

867. Tennis star Chris Evert.

No.

MISCELLANEOUS

Q

868. Who was the coach of the 1973-74 American Basketball Association's San Diego Conquistadors?

Wilt Chamberlain.

869. Which four ABA teams were absorbed into the NBA?

Indiana Pacers, Denver Nuggets, New Jersey Nets and San Antonio Spurs.

870. Name three of the five players banned from the NBA that played in the ABA.

Roger Brown, Connie Hawkins, Tony Jackson, Doug Moe and Charlie Williams.

871. Mike Storen, general manager of the ABA's Kentucky and Indiana teams, had a child become a national sportscaster. Name the sportscaster.

Hannah Storm.

872. What classmate was Willie Wise's best friend when he attended City College of San Francisco?

O.J. Simpson.

873. What NBA all-star had to sit out a year when he left the Atlanta Hawks and signed with the Los Angeles Stars?

Zelmo Beaty.

874. What pop singer owned the Oakland Oaks?

Pat Boone.

875. What network announcer after graduating from Syracuse began his professional career as the radio announcer of the Spirits of St. Louis?

Bob Costas.

876. Adolph Rupp was president of what ABA team?

Memphis Tams.

877. Who owned the Memphis Tams?

Charles Finley.

878. And what did Tams stand for?

Tennessee, Arkansas and Mississippi.

879. What were the only three ABA franchises that never moved?

Indiana, Denver, Kentucky.

880. Who was the first ABA commissioner?

George Mikan.

881. Who was the last ABA commissioner?

Dave DeBusschere.

882. Instead of retiring a uniform number, how did the Boston Celtics honor broadcaster Johnny Most?

They "retired" his microphone.

883. What long-time Philadelphia public address announcer also had a microphone retired in his honor?

Dave Zinkoff.

884. In an episode of *Seinfeld*, Cosmo Kramer describes attending an NBA game and getting into a fight with which player?

Reggie Miller.

885. In *The Absent-Minded Professor*, what did Fred MacMurray attach flubber to in order for his college team to win?

The players' shoes.

886. In what 1979 film did Julius Erving appear?

The Fish That Saved Pittsburgh.

887. In what movie did Alex English make his acting debut?

Amazing Grace and Chuck.

888. What befell Kareem Abdul-Jabbar in *Airplane*?

Food poisoning.

889. What fictional high school won the Indiana state championship in *Hoosiers*?

Hickory.

890. What actor played the coach of Hickory High?

Gene Hackman.

891. Milan (Indiana) High School (the real Hickory High) beat Indianapolis Crispus Attucks in the state final. Who was the star player of Attucks?

Oscar Robertson.

892. What basketball documentary won several major awards in 1994, but was snubbed by the Academy Awards?

Hoop Dreams.

893. What NBA player was featured in *My Giant*?

Gheorghe Muresan.

894. What was Billy Crystal's occupation in *Forget Paris*?

NBA referee.

895. What NBA player shares a name with the Tin Man?

Jack Haley.

Who Were the Subjects in These Basketball Biographies?

896. *I Love Being the Enemy.* Bob Knight, Reggie Miller or Latrell Sprewell?

Reggie Miller.

897. *Bad As I Wanna Be.* Dennis Rodman, Charles Barkley or Rick Mahorn?

Dennis Rodman.

898. *Best Seat In the House.* Phil Jackson, Spike Lee or Jack Nicholson?

Spike Lee.

899. *Pressed For Success.* Bob Huggins, Press Maravich or Pat Riley?

Bob Huggins.

900. *Change the Game: One Athlete's Thoughts on Sports, Dreams, and Growing Up.* Shaquille O'Neal, David Robinson or Grant Hill?

Grant Hill.

901. *Winning by His Grace.* Charlie Ward, Mark Price or John Stockton.

Charlie Ward.

902. *Breaking Barriers.* Rebecca Lobo, Clem Haskins or Bill Russell?

Clem Haskins.

903. *Drive: The Story of My Life.* Larry Bird, Magic Johnson or Isiah Thomas?

Larry Bird.

904. *For the Love of the Game.* Karl Malone, Rick Pitino or Michael Jordan?

Michael Jordan.

905. *Tower of Power.* Patrick Ewing, Ralph Sampson or Hakeem Olajuwon?

Hakeem Olajuwon.

906. In 1971 East Chicago Washington was 29-0 and won the Indiana state championship. All five starters went on to play in college. Name three of those stars and their schools.

Junior Bridgeman, Louisville; Pete Trgovich, UCLA; Pete Stoddard, North Carolina State; Ruben Bailey, Montana State; and Darnell Adell, Murray State.

907. Who is taller, Gheorge Muresan or Shawn Bradley?

Muresan is 7-foot-7, Bradley is 7-foot-6.

908. Who is taller, Muggsy Bogues or Monte Towe?

Towe at 5-foot-6 towers over Bogues at 5-foot-3.

909. Who is eligible for the Frances Pomeroy Naismith Award?

Any NCAA player under 6-feet tall.

910. Why is the Naismith Basketball Hall of Fame located in Springfield, Massachusetts?

To honor Dr. James Naismith who invented basketball in that city in 1891.

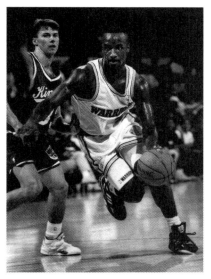

Vincent Askew

911. What famous Hall of Fame football coach also is a member of the Naismith Basketball Hall of Fame?

Amos Alonzo Stagg.

912. How many years must a player be retired to be eligible for the Hall of Fame?

Five.

913. Who are the only players to win two CBA Most Valuable Player awards?

Vincent Askew and Charlie Criss.

914. Which of these players did not play for the Harlem Globetrotters? Wilt Chamberlain, Hal Greer or Connie Hawkins?

Hal Greer.

915. Who was the commissioner of the American Basketball League?

Globetrotters owner Abe Saperstein.

916. Name four of the eight cities that had an ABL team in 1961-62.

New York, Chicago, Pittsburgh, Cleveland, Los Angeles, San Francisco, Kansas City and Honolulu.

917. What team won the only ABL championship?

Cleveland.

918. Julius Erving and Bill Cosby are partners in what business?

A Philadelphia Coca-Cola bottler and distributor.

919. Magic Johnson owned a radio station in what state?

Colorado.

920. What person has been involved in the most NBA games as a player and/or coach?

Lenny Wilkens.

921. Who is second on the list of most NBA games as a player or coach?

Don Nelson.

922. What oil company sponsored the AAU team with the most national titles?

Phillips.

923. What was significant about a basketball game played at Birmingham V.A. Hospital at Van Nuys, California, in 1946?

It was the first wheelchair basketball game played.

924. What is the name of the summer league in Philadelphia frequented by pros and top collegians?

Baker League.

925. What was the name of the semi-pro team financed by singer Kate Smith?

Kate Smith's Celtics.

Match these mascots with their NBA team:

926. Hugo	a. Phoenix
927. Boomer	b. Charlotte
928. Benny	c. Miami
929. Gorilla	d. Indiana
930. Coyote	e. Utah
931. Harry	f. San Antonio
932. Rocky	g. Atlanta
933. Bango	h. Milwaukee
934. Bear	i. Chicago
935. Burnie	j. Denver

926. b, 927. d, 928. i, 929. a, 930. f, 931. g, 932. j, 933. h, 934. e, 935. c.

936. Who was the "World's Greatest Dribbler" that spent more than 40 years with the Harlem Globetrotters and his own Harlem Magicians?

Marques "The Magician" Haynes.

937. What team perennially loses to the Harlem Globetrotters?

Washington Generals.

938. Who was the long suffering coach of the Generals?

Red Klotz.

939. Who was the first female Globetrotter?

Lynette Woodard.

940. Who are the only three players to win championships in high school, college, the NBA and Olympics?

Quinn Buckner, Magic Johnson and Jerry Lucas.

941. What was the nickname of the CBA team based in Puerto Rico from 1983-85?

Coquis.

942. What NBA Hall of Famer coached Wilmington for two years in the Eastern Basketball League?

Neil Johnston.

943. Who was the first 7-footer to play in the National Junior College Tournament?

Artis Gilmore of Gardner-Webb, North Carolina.

944. Before his parents could complete their immigration from Russia to the U.S., World War II intervened. What NBA player spent six years as a child in a Japanese concentration camp?

Tom Meschery.

945. In 1923 the rules were changed so that free throws had to be shot by the player who was fouled, rather than the previous practice of what?

Having the team's most accurate shooter attempt them all.

946. Long before the NBA, pro basketball was dominated by three independent, traveling teams. Name "The Team of the Decade" for the 1910s, 1920s and 1930s.

1910s: Buffalo Germans, 1920s: Original Celtics (of New York), and 1930s: Harlem Renaissance Big Five (Rens).

947. What organization was considered the first professional league?

National League of 1898-99 with teams in Philadelphia, Trenton, Millville, Camden, Hancock and Germantown.

948. Who was Michael Jordan's minor league baseball major that now is managing in the big leagues?

Terry Francona.

949. What is the largest crowd to ever watch a high school basketball game?

41,101 which watched the 1990 Indiana state final in the RCA Dome.

950. After scoring a national high school record with 135 points in 1960, Danny Heater never played another game. Why?

He had a scholarship to Richmond, but was involved in an auto accident and was not physically able to compete again.

951. What future Blue Devil and NBA player broke Calvin Murphy's high school scoring records in Connecticut?

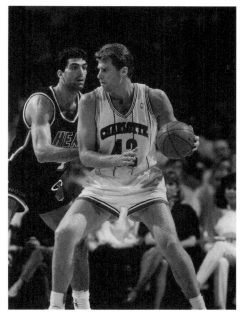

Mike Gminski

Mike Gminski.

952. Where did Bobby Hurley play high school basketball under his father, Bob?

St. Anthony of Jersey City (N.J.).

953. What baseball team owner once owned the Cleveland Pipers in the ABL?

George Steinbrenner.

954. Who was the first player to go directly from high school to the pros?

Moses Malone.

955. Why was Hank Luisetti suspended for a year by the AAU?

He was paid $10,000 for appearing with Betty Grable in the movie Campus Confessions.

956. Michael Jordan returned to North Carolina to complete his college degree. What was his major field of study?

Geography.

957. When did the game stop having jump balls after every basket?

1937.

958. Besides basketball, what other sport was invented in Springfield, Massachusetts?

Volleyball.

959. Who are the four players who went from an NCAA championship team to an NBA championship the following year?

Bill Russell, Henry Bibby, Magic Johnson and Billy Thompson.

960. Who was the first player to win titles in college, the NBA and Olympics?

Clyde Lovellette.

961. Who is the only current NBA player born on Leap Year Day (Feb. 29)?

Chucky Brown.

John Lucas

962. What planet did Darryl Dawkins claim to be from?

Lovetron.

963. Who was the only World Team Tennis player to play in the NBA?

John Lucas.

964. Name one of the three NBA referees to work a record five all-star games.

Darryl Garretson, Jake O'Donnell and Ed T. Rush.

965. Who are the only two members of the Naismith Basketball Hall of Fame in the both the players and coaches wings?

Lenny Wilkens and John Wooden.

966. In what four countries have the NBA played regular season games?

U.S., Canada, Japan and Mexico.

967. How long is an NBA playing court?

94 feet.

968. How wide is an NBA backboard?

6 feet.

969. How far is the NBA three-point line at the farthest point?

23-feet-9 inches to the center of the basket.

970. When is an NBA game in "the final two minutes?" When the clock reads 2:00 or 1:59?

2:00.

971. How much is the fine for using STICK-UM in an NBA game?

$25.

972. Who is the NBA championship trophy named in honor of?

Larry O'Brien.

973. What's the earliest date the NBA Finals have been concluded?

April 7 (in 1956).

974. Dr. James Naismith had 13 original rules of basketball. What is the first rule?

The ball may be thrown in any direction with one or both hands.

975. How long is an NBA halftime?

14 minutes.

976. What school was the first to have both its men's and women's teams advance to the NCAA Final Four in the same year?

Georgia in 1983.

977. What school was the first to have both its men's and women's teams ranked No. 1 in the polls simultaneously?

Connecticut in 1995.

978. Who is the last NCAA scoring champion to play in an NBA all-star game?

Hersey Hawkins.

979. Who is the last NCAA rebounding champion to play in an NBA all-star game?

Tim Duncan.

980. Who is the last NCAA assists leader to play in an NBA all-star game?

Jason Kidd.

981. When was the last time an NBA team failed to have anyone score in double figures?

1950, Ft. Wayne vs. Minneapolis.

982. Where is the 2002 World Basketball Championship scheduled to be played?

Indianapolis, Indiana.

983. Who are the only two players to win NCAA, NIT and NBA championships?

Tom Gola and Arnie Ferrin.

984. Who is the only person to have a brother and son play in the NBA?

Al McGuire whose brother was Dick and son was Allie.

985. True or False. Tom Lasorda was a referee in the Continental Basketball Association.

True, when it was known as the Eastern Basketball League.

986. Who played in the 1946 World Series after appearing in 11 games in the National Basketball League?

Del Rice.

987. Where did the NCAA administrative offices move to in 1999?

Indianapolis, Indiana.

988. Where did the National Federation of High Schools move to in 1999?

Indianapolis, Indiana.

989. True or False? NBA officials wear black and white striped shirts.

False.

990. In what country was Dr. James Naismith born?

Canada.

Match the first and last names on this "All-French" team:

991. Joubert, Michigan   a. Jacque
992. Wilkens, Georgia   b. Antoine
993. Miller, Utah   c. Lafayette
994. Vaughn, Kansas   d. Dominique
995. Lever, Arizona State   e. Andre

658. b, 659. d, 660. e, 661. a, 662. c.

996. What long-time ABA coach made the free throw which won the 1953 NCAA championship game?

Bob Leonard, Indiana.

997. Where was the first high school to accumulate 1,500 basketball victories?

Centralia, Illinois.

998. Name the three NBA players from Macon (Ga.) Southwest High School.

Norm Nixon, Jeff Malone and Sharone Wright.

999. What did Wilt Chamberlain call his dream house that he had built in the Santa Monica Mountains?

Ursa Major (The Big Dipper).

1,000. Who is the only NBA player to have his uniform number retired before he completed his career?

Michael Jordan, #23.

1,001. What Washington, D.C., fan had an NBA rule named in his honor that is designed to keep hostile crowds from interfering with a team's huddle during timeouts?

Robin Ficker.

Other Basketball
Related Sports Publishing Titles

Hot Rod Hundley: "You Gotta Love it Baby!"

by Rod Hundley with Tom McEachin

Rod Hundley announces Jazz games on radio, TV, and cable and he has the unique distinction of being the only announcer in Jazz history. Rod's unique style and familiar voice have made him one of the most popular and well-recognized broadcasters in the business today. His broadcasting career includes stints with the New Orleans Jazz, Los Angeles Lakers, and the Phoenix Suns. A three-year All-American at West Virginia, Hundley was the first pick of the 1957 NBA College draft by Cincinnati.

1998 • 275 pp • 6 x 9 hardcover • ISBN 1-57167-243-5 • $22.95

Also available in limited leatherbound edition

Limited to 500 copies. Signed by Rod Hundley, John Stockton, Jerry West and Connie Hawkins.

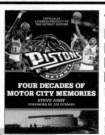

The Detroit Pistons: Four Decades of Motor City Memories

by Steve Addy

During the 40 years that the Pistons have made their home in Detroit, the franchise has spanned the spectrum of success, from years of frustration to back-to-back NBA championships.
This team-endorsed publication includes easy-to-read stories and hundreds of photographs, many that have never been circulated to the general public.
Players from all decades are featured, including Dave DeBusschere in the '50s and '60s to Dave Bing and Bob Lanier in the '70s to Isiah Thomas and Grant Hill in the '80s and '90s.

1997 • 263 pp • 8 1/2 x 11 hardcover • ISBN 1-57167-144-7 • $39.95

Also available in limited leatherbound edition

Limited to 500 copies. Signed by Bill Laimbeer, Rick Mahorn, Kelly Tripucka and Kent Benson. $99.95

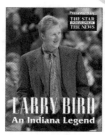

Larry Bird: An Indiana Legend

Throughout his basketball career, Larry Bird has gathered countless accolades and awards. From Springs Valley High School to Indiana State University to the Boston Celtics to the Indiana Pacers, one thing has remained the same: Bird's commitment to excellence. Drawn from the archives of the Indianapolis Star/News, Larry Bird: An Indiana Legend traces Bird's basketball journey from his days as a high school standout through his outstanding season as the rookie head coach of the Pacers, including his days at Indiana State and his stellar career with the Celtics.

1998 • 185 pp • 8 1/2 x 11 hardcover • ISBN 1-58261-008-8 • $29.95

Available at your local bookstore or by calling 877-424-2665